Cheshire Vol II

Edited by Heather Killingray

YoungWriters
First published in Great Britain in 2006 by:
Young Writers
Remus House
Coltsfoot Drive
Peterborough
PE2 9JX
Telephone: 01733 890066
Website: www.youngwriters.co.uk

SB ISBN 1 84602 540 0

Foreword

Imagine a teenager's brain; a fertile yet fragile expanse teeming with ideas, aspirations, questions and emotions. Imagine a classroom full of racing minds, scratching pens writing an endless stream of ideas and thoughts . . .

. . . Imagine your words in print reaching a wider audience. Imagine that maybe, just maybe, your words can make a difference. Strike a chord. Touch a life. Change the world. Imagine no more . . .

'I Have a Dream' is a series of poetry collections written by 11 to 18-year-olds from schools and colleges across the UK and overseas. Pupils were invited to send us their poems using the theme 'I Have a Dream'. Selected entries range from dreams they've experienced to childhood fantasies of stardom and wealth, through inspirational poems of their dreams for a better future and of people who have influenced and inspired their lives.

The series is a snapshot of who and what inspires, influences and enthuses young adults of today. It shows an insight into their hopes, dreams and aspirations of the future and displays how their dreams are an escape from the pressures of today's modern life. Young Writers are proud to present this anthology, which is truly inspired and sure to be an inspiration to all who read it.

Contents

The Poems

I Have A Dream

I have a dream
That one day
The world will be a better place.

I have a dream
That one day
Pollution will no longer exist.

I have a dream
That one day
The human race will live in harmony.

I have a dream
That one day
Global warming will be a thing of the past.

I have a dream
That one day
Poverty really will be history.

I have a dream
That today
This will start to take place.

Emma O'Connor (11)
Penketh High School

I Have A Dream

I have a dream that in my world
There will be no bullying.

I have a dream that in my world
There will be no poverty.

I have a dream that in my world
There will be no uniform worn at school.

I have a dream that in my world
People will never go without money.

I have a dream that in my world
Poor people will all have a home, food and drink.

Sophie Hankey (13)
Penketh High School

I Have A Dream

I have a dream
The world could be the happy place you love.

I have a dream
The day will come when Man stands down and ends all war.

I have a dream
The world could get along.

I have a dream
Difference made no sense.

I have a dream
Poverty didn't exist.

I have a dream
Everyone is equal

I have a dream
No one will be cruel or offensive.

I have a dream
The world could sit with the flowers
And the grass under the trees
Like it was so many years ago.

I have a dream
Global warming doesn't mean anything.

I have a dream,
But it's only a dream . . .

Hannah Smith (12)
Penketh High School

I Have A Dream

I have a dream
There will be peace among people,
But some people don't.
I have a dream
There should be no wars,
But some people don't.
I have a dream
That everyone will be treated as equal,
But some people don't.
These people in the world
Have a dream
Which consists only of violence,
Which consists only of evil.

I have a dream,
Theodore Roosevelt had a dream,
Martin Luther King Jr had a dream,
Mohamed Anwar Al-Sadat had a dream,
Mother Teresa had a dream,
Aung San Suu Kyi had a dream,
Nelson Mandela and former President Frederik Willem de Klerk
had a dream
Yasser Arafat, Shimon Peres and Yitzhak Rabin had a dream,
John Hume and David Trimble had a dream,
Wangari Maathai had a dream,
We all have a dream,
Let's make it reality.

Matthew Berry (12)
Penketh High School

I Have A Dream

I saw them falling,
I heard them crying,
And yes, I saw them dying.

I heard them calling,
I saw them beating,
I saw them pointing,
I heard them crying,
And yes, I saw them cowering.

I saw them throwing,
I saw the smoke rising,
And yes, I saw the waters darkening.

I saw them cutting,
I heard them cry, 'Timber'.

I saw them killing,
I heard them screaming,
And yes, I saw them dying.

I have seen and heard:
War, racism, pollution,
Destruction of the rainforest, animal cruelty.

I have seen and heard it all.
I don't want to see and hear any more!

Shelby Walker (11)
Penketh High School

I Have A Dream

I have a dream that racism will stop
And the amount of pollution will start to drop.

I have a dream that there is no crime
And wars will stop in no time.

I have a dream that nobody is poor,
And having no cigarettes is the law.

James Kennedy (11)
Penketh High School

What Is The Dream?

What is the dream?
Is it peace throughout the world?
Is it happiness as well?
Is it freedom, liberty?
Is that the dream?

What is the dream?
Is it children?
Is it their safety?
Is it the joy we can create?
Is that the dream?

What is the dream?
Is it no poverty?
Is it no suffering?
Is it to be free from harm?
Is that the dream?

What is the dream?
Is it no pollution?
Is it beauty in the world?
Is it kindness to each other?
Is that the dream?

What is the dream?
Children are the dream,
Freedom is the dream,
The future is the dream.
We are the dream.

Rebecca Rowland (11)
Penketh High School

I Have A Dream

I have a dream that poverty comes to an end!
I have a dream that smoking goes round the bend.
I have a dream that racism goes away.
I have a dream that crime doesn't stay.

Neil Carver (12)
Penketh High School

I Have A Dream

I have a dream of
Happiness and peace,
No racism will ever be
Called out in the street.
Cruelty to animals
Will be banned,
Pollution will fall into hand.
Illness and addiction
Will be no more,
No one will ever
Again be poor.
This is a dream
I do demand,
So come on everyone,
Let's get crime banned.

Hannah E Jones (12)
Penketh High School

I Have A Dream

I have a dream . . .
That peace will be made,
Our love will be shared
For all that we gain.

I have a dream . . .
That racism will stop,
We'll all be ourselves,
Not something we're not.

I have a dream . . .
That cruelty to animals will stop,
They will be treated as humans,
Even though they are not.

Mica Stockton (11)
Penketh High School

Words To Change The World

Imagine
A world with no crime.
Imagine
Not having to lock the door for fear of being robbed.
Imagine
A world with no wars.
Imagine
A world with no guns, bombs or fighting.
Imagine
A world with no poverty.
Imagine
A world with no pollution.
Imagine
The air being clean and breathable.
Imagine
A world with no disease.
Imagine
Nobody being ill and humans keeping their numbers.
Imagine
A world with no bad drugs.
Imagine
A world where people are not in constant pain.
Imagine!

Sam Sant (12)
Penketh High School

Dream

D is for danger that crime has created.
R is for river that science has polluted.
E is for Earth where everyone's dying.
A is for Africa where poverty is.
M is for marijuana, one of the addictive drugs.

Thomas Goulding (11)
Penketh High School

Think Of The World

Think of the world
Where black and white
Will all get along and not start a fight.

Think of the world
With dogs and cats
Not locked up or turned into hats.

Think of the world
With freedom in life,
No war in Iraq or dead with a knife.

Think of the world
Where poverty is history,
No children are starved and food is a mystery.

Think of the world
With peace and tranquillity,
Everyone that we meet is full of humility.

Charlotte Bates (12)
Penketh High School

I Have A Dream

I have a dream with no hurt and no bleeding,
I have a dream with no war with any meaning.

I have a dream with no hunger, no dying,
I have a dream with no tears and no crying.

I have a dream, you have one too,
To make the world better for me and you.

I have a dream,
Do you have yours?

Katherine Stephenson
Penketh High School

Words To Change The World

I once had a dream
I was in a new world,
A world where I could make a difference,
A world where I was happy.

I was in a world without . . .
Poverty or racism,
No wars and no crime,
A world where everyone was treated equally
And not judged by their colour.

I often stand and wonder why
This world we live in is like it is
And why.

Ellen Bleasdale (12)
Penketh High School

My Dream - World Peace

I have a dream and it's probably the same
As many other dreams,
The world is peaceful and
The wars have all ceased.

Children's laughter fills the air as I dream on
In this peaceful world,
The thundering bombs and firing of guns
Are a long, distant nightmare.

People now live in harmony, with love,
Peace and respect for each other.
As the day is dawning, I am waking,
Please God, don't take away my dream.

Daniel Sillery (12)
Penketh High School

Do You Dream?

Do you dream
That no one's dreaming your dream?
Do you dream
To make the world a better place,
Stop all the abuse and poverty?
Do you dream
To stop the fights,
Make the pain go away?
Do you dream
That every child should have parents
To look after them and keep them safe?
Do you dream
That every illness can be cured
Or that this stupid world is ever going to change?
Do you dream
That everyone is going to be happy
Or is everyone and everything going to be the same?
Do you dream
That you are standing alone, with no one by your side?

Chloe Price (12)
Penketh High School

I Have A Dream

I have a dream that everything is right,
People are friends and nobody will fight.

I have a dream to keep people alive,
Make them feel happy and good inside.

I have a dream that love is all around,
Keeping people together and making us proud.

I have a dream that illness is gone,
Helping to make people live on.

Jack Holt (12)
Penketh High School

I Dream . . .

No dream is ever too big,
No dream is ever too small,
No dream is ever wrong,
No dream is ever impossible.

In my dream there is a world,
A world without racism,
A world without cruelty.

In my dream I am alone,
I wonder why the world is cruel,
I wonder why the world is mean.

In my dream there is a child
With arms wrapped around her,
With love coming from all around,
She is safe!

Think, what do you dream?

Robyn Lunt
Penketh High School

I Have A Dream

I have a dream
Homes aren't wrecked
And animals are not scared.
Various religions will not be forgotten,
Everyone counts
And an old person should not be treated differently.
Do what you want, not what your friends want,
Real things should matter.
Earth is a nice place.
A child should live a happy life.
My dream is this.

Amy Dagnall (11)
Penketh High School

Words To Change The World

Sometimes I wonder why the world is like it is,
With all the war and poverty, and arguing over that and this.
Sometimes I am alone, just crying by myself,
When I've taken all my dreams away and put them on the shelf.
But although I'm hurt inside, I always stop and think,
What if I took away my problems and washed them down the sink?

So take away your problems and then there sat beside you
Are all the things you've always had, like love that burns inside you.
And with your problems gone, you can start to build your dreams,
To help all of us make the world more than it seems.
So come along with me and bring your friends as well,
For if we come together, we can destroy this living hell.

So watch out everyone,
Because here we come.
Yes, we're going to help the human race,
To make the world a better place!

Anna Loftus (11)
Penketh High School

I Wish

I wish for world peace, do you?
I wish for gun crime around the
World to stop, do you?
I wish for no more murders
Because of people's religions, do you?
I wish that child abuse would stop, do you?
I wish people would get more credit
For trying to make a change, do you?

Do you want all this? I do!

Danny Vernon (11)
Penketh High School

I Have A Dream That . . .

P eople can unite, black or white, rich or poor,
O thers smile at the help you can give,
V ery little amounts of money and food are asked for,
E very race and every human should live without poverty,
R especting that you have a lot more than some people,
T oday, tomorrow, people in poverty will suffer,
Y ou have maybe heard the song?

'H elping all the people . . .'
I t talks about poverty,
S o we're here to make poverty *history!*
T ogether we can,
O nly think that in the space of three seconds someone dies
from poverty.

R eally you can help our human race,
Y ou can make a difference and make poverty history!

Ashlea Brogan
Penketh High School

I Have A Dream

I have a dream
And it might be the same
As what other people dream,
But I would like to spread the message
That all across the world,
Where people live in peace and harmony,
And that sickness and hunger
Will come to pass.
I have this dream.

Cuen Keller (11)
Penketh High School

My Ideal World

My ideal world is probably
Quite alike to yours.

My ideal world
Is a world where
People are nice to each other
And there's no racism.

My ideal world
Is a world where people
Look after the elderly.

My ideal world
Is a world where people
Do not abuse their children.

My ideal world
Is a world where people
Can live, not worrying about
Wars and bombings.

My ideal world
Is a world where
People make sure the hospitals
And care homes are clean and tidy.

My ideal world
Is a world where
People are kind and considerate.

My ideal world
Is a world where
People can visit other countries
Without worrying about terrorism.

My ideal world
Is a world where people
Can live in peace and harmony.

My ideal world
Is a world where every public place
Is a non-smoking zone.

My ideal world
Is a world
Without crime.

Is my ideal world alike to yours?

Sophie Bailey (11)
Penketh High School

My Dream

I dream that the world
Will be a better place,
Where people aren't judged
By their religion or race.

I dreamt I could walk
Around every day
And see people being treated
The same way.

I dream that people
Will not cause a war,
Lots of people die,
Both the rich and the poor.

I dream that people
Will help each other out,
If people were homeless
Or a place had a drought.

I dream there are no
Villains or thugs,
Damaging property
Or dealing drugs.

I just want the world
To be happy and clean,
That is my poem.
That is my dream.

Thomas Nicholas (12)
Penketh High School

Imagine

Imagine
A world of peace.
Imagine
A world with no wars.
Imagine
A place with no fighting and conflict.
Imagine an Earth with everybody as friends.
Imagine
A world with no murders.
Imagine
A world with no crime and theft.
Imagine
A place with no jealousy.
Imagine
Somewhere where nothing bad happens to people.
Imagine.

Michael Lakeland (12)
Penketh High School

Optimism

Beauty grasps onto the flower
As it dies and decays,
Love is in the eye of the beholder
And grows in the sun's bright rays.

Peace follows mankind
Every step of his journey,
Freedom covers the Earth,
It is there late and early.

Nicole Segar (12)
Penketh High School

Dreams

Do you dream of a peaceful world
With no fighting?
Do you dream of a world
Where no one hates or fights?
Do you dream that everyone is equal?
Do you dream to stop
Racism and abuse?

Fight for freedom, peace,
Fairness and safety.

Oliver Lewis (12)
Penketh High School

George Best

(1946-2005)

He was born in the north of Ireland, Belfast to be exact,
And there was a United scout who saw his talent and reported back.

So he flew over to England to show his true colours,
Busby was so pleased George joined the Man U brothers.

Under Busby's management,
The United fans saw George's raw talent.

George's display
Got him really good pay.

He got hot chicks
And a car to match his tricks.

He quit United after intense pressure,
So he moved to Spain to get peace and pleasure.

He may have done bad things in his life like drinking beer,
But he made it up by giving his fans a really loud cheer.

His time is now up; his football years are gone,
We will never forget him because he was United's number *one!*

Thomas Smyth (12)
Priestnall School

My Inspiration

(Children in Need)

I turned on my telly
To 'Children in Need',
Campaigning for viewers to do a good deed.

They were asking for money
For children in need,
And hoping that viewers would take heed.

They were showing clips
Of children in need,
Tempting viewers to do a good deed.

This made me donate
Towards 'Children in Need',
Showing that I had taken heed.

Philip Kemp (13)
Priestnall School

I Dream

Dreams of a different world,
Dreams of no hurt, no sorrow,
No crime or poverty,
Just a perfect world.
We can change the world,
But being willing is not enough.
We have to go out and take action.
Obstacles can be
Stepping stones to our dreams.
We shouldn't give up
After we get knocked down,
We should carry on
Because one day it *will* happen!
Our dreams can come true
But only if we work hard enough
To make them real.

Jessica Coombs (13)
Priestnall School

I Dream

I dream of a different world,
Without any pain or sorrow.
I dream of a different world
For today and for tomorrow.

I dream of a different world,
No racism, no discrimination.
I dream of a different world
For today and the next generation.

I dream of a different world
Where everyone is equal.
I dream of a different world,
Full of happy people.

I dream of a different world
Full of hope and joy.
I dream of a different world
For every girl and boy.

I dream of a different world
For you and for me.
I dream of a different world
For everyone to see.

Elizabeth Ayres (12)
Priestnall School

I Have A Dream

The world can change in every way,
Aliens might come down from space,
More and more people die from disease,
Kids learning at school for free.

The world needs to change,
It can be a better place.
There's too much crime
And too little time.

Will Marsh (13)
Priestnall School

Don't Judge

(A poem inspired by Martin Luther King)

You judge by religion,
You judge by race,
You judge by skin colour
And the look of someone's face.

Who are you to say what someone is
Without looking for the person inside?
Ignoring their opinions, ignoring their thoughts,
Like personality is meant to hide.

In this world we shouldn't be judged or grouped,
This world is meant to share,
Not to say your thoughts are wrong,
But neither are they fair.

Don't judge by religion,
Don't judge by race,
Don't judge by skin colours,
Because it's not your place.

Yasmin Clayson (12)
Priestnall School

The World Should Be A Better Place

The world should be a better place
Where people don't judge people
By how they act or their race
The world should be a better place.

The world should learn to share
Because being greedy
Is not fair
The world should learn to share.

People should not fight
Because beating people up
Is not right
People should not fight.

George Hodgetts (13)
Priestnall School

Friends

Friends, friends, they're the best,
But always put you to the test.
I love them loads
And everyone knows
They are my inspiration
And inspire the whole nation.

When I am down my friends are there
And show me that they care.
My best friend is Kate,
Because she is a great mate!
My other friends are just as important,
The thing that brought us together is fate.

They are always having a laugh,
Even if the joke is naff.
This poem is about my friends
And I hope our friendship never ends!

Chloe Smith (12)
Priestnall School

Kurt Cobain

When he set foot upon stage,
With his guitar in hand,
He stood in front of a roaring crowd
With the rest of his outstanding band.

Ready to rock the house down
With a chart-topping song,
In a sold-out concert,
He will rock all day long.

All around the world,
City by city,
He will leave them all speechless
With his music, hard and gritty.

Adam Moores (12)
Priestnall School

I Have A Dream

I have a dream
To let the world be.
I have a dream
That everyone can see.

I have a dream
To stop world hunger.
I have a dream
On what people wonder . . .

I have a dream
To stop all wars.
I have a dream
To hear no more.

I have a dream
To help Africa.
I have a dream
To show you what Africa is.

I have a dream
To change the law.
I had a dream
That no one saw.

I have a dream
To feed the poor.
I have a dream
To give them more.

I have a dream
To share with the rich.
I have a dream
To share with the poor.

I have a dream
That crime will stop.
I have a dream
That we won't hear another gunshot pop.

So here's a poem
From me to you,
Just top and think
What everyone could do!

Megan Shields (12)
Priestnall School

The Thing That Inspires Me The Most

I feel really grim
When they walk past
They are all wrinkly,
As if wearing a mask.

They walk so slow
And waddle along,
You can't imagine them
Wearing a thong.

They have bad taste,
Especially in clothes.
They dress like
Old scabby toes.

I know I have been going on
And saying all this nasty stuff,
But the thing really is,
Even though some are a tizz,
I love them,
Like loads.

I wish all mine were here,
But I know they will always be near.
I love old people
And that's why they inspire me the most.

Emma Williams (13)
Priestnall School

This World

In this small, small world,
There is a continent.
In that small, small continent,
There is a country.
In that small, small country
There is a war.
In that small, small war
There is a church.
In that small, small church
There is a mass grave.
In that mass, mass grave
There is an innocent child.

In this mad, mad world
There are bad, bad people
Who make this world
A terrible place.

In this world there is chaos and lies,
Seems the only thing growing
Is the terror inside.

But when people hurt and people cry,
Family and friends make their spirits fly.

In this chaotic and terrible world,
One thing always takes place,
Not your looks or popularity,
But the smile on your face.

Jack Cunningham (12)
Priestnall School

Cancer Research UK

It started a few years ago,
I think I was just eight,
My auntie went to the hospital and said,
'Doctor, my eye aches.'

After a few tests
They finally had an answer.
They sent my auntie a letter which said,
'Sorry, you've got eye cancer.'

My family was distraught,
It certainly wasn't planned,
Little did we know
There was a helping hand.

They're called Cancer Research UK,
I bet you've heard of them,
But without the kind guys down there,
She would have gone to bedlam.

After a few weeks,
I went to go and see her,
And when I asked the doctors,
They said she was getting better.

After about six months,
At last they let her out.
Without them at Cancer Research UK,
She would have died, no doubt.

So here's a little hint
To send you on your way,
Give all the money you can
To Cancer Research UK.

Alice Tweats (13)
Priestnall School

Rosa Parks

She stood up by sitting down
When on a bus coming from town.
A woman who inspires me a lot,
Rosa Parks wanted respect that everyone got.

There was only a slight difference between her and everyone,
She wanted rights but she got none.
She was black and everyone was white,
There wasn't equal respect and that wasn't right.

Rosa Parks wanted to do something good,
By making black people get the same respect
As white people would.
She did so much for an equal right,
She made the country be united, black and white.

Hannah Wiseman (12)
Priestnall School

I Have A Dream

I have a dream, my thoughts at night,
An end to racism,
Is that our right?

Black or white, both the same,
Killing each other,
It's not a game.

White or black, I couldn't care,
Both are people,
We must be fair.

Attitudes change, whatever race,
Tolerance, knowledge,
Soon to be a better place.

Callum Hampson (13)
Priestnall School

I Have A Dream

I have a dream
For a world full of peace,
No fights, no war,
Just friendship and love.

I have a dream
Of a world with no racism,
With white and black children
Who will play with each other.

I have a dream
When things go wrong,
To start a new day,
Turn over a new leaf.

I have a dream
For a world of equality,
For people not to be rich,
But not to be poor.

I have a dream
For people to love,
For people to care,
For people to have a love of their own.

I have a dream
Of no disease,
No illness,
No death . . .

I have a dream
For people to like you
For who you are,
Not what you've got.

I have a dream
For my perfect world,
My perfect dream.

Daniel Johnson (12)
Priestnall School

I Have A Dream

Everyone should be equal,
Nobody should be mistreated,
For everyone is the same.
We should all be united.

In a small country
There is a big war,
Where people die more and more.

Some people make this world so bad,
With all the bombings in Baghdad.
All the world should get along,
So let's be friends for very long.

This is how the world should be,
A safer place for you and me.
Let's put those nasty people away,
We should find a safer place to stay.

Daniel Child (12)
Priestnall School

I Have A Dream

People lost their hope,
Lost their love,
Died in the war.

Some will cry,
Lose their family,
Die in the war.

Some losing their friends,
Losing their smile,
Dying in the war.

But I will never lose my dream,
The dream in which the war is over,
No more war in the world,
Because I have a dream.

Grace Kim (13)
Priestnall School

I Have A Dream

I have a dream
To stop the gunshots,
To stop the screams,
I have a dream.

I have a dream
Which I hope comes true.
I have a dream
And so should you.

In my dream
No one gets shot,
No one screams,
That's only in my dream.

I have a dream
Which I hope comes true.
I have a dream
And so should you.

I have a dream
To find out why people are mean,
To find out how to stop them,
I have a dream.

I have a dream
Which I hope comes true.
I have a dream
And so should you.

In my dream
I find out why people are mean,
I find out how to stop them,
That's only in my dream.

I have a dream
Which I hope comes true.
I have a dream
And so should you!

Sadie Halstead (12)
Priestnall School

I Have A Dream

I have a dream
That there is nothing bad
And the world is a team,
Then no one would be sad.

Do people have to be poor?
Not if people shared.
I wish there wasn't any war,
Then people wouldn't be scared.

There is a lot of crime,
People killed or hurt.
It happens all the time,
People falling to the dirt.

Lots of people are wealthy,
Lots of money they could share,
When people are in poverty,
They don't even care.

I have a dream
That there is peace,
That the world is a team,
I have a dream . . .

Alice Williams (12)
Priestnall School

I Have A Dream

Score a goal, I score a goal,
Everybody cheering in the crowd,
Everybody clapping all around.
I have a dream to play for my favourite team,
I have a dream to move like a beam,
I have a dram to score the winning goal,
I have a dream not to hit the pole.
I have a dream to be a star,
I have a dream to run so far,
I have a dream to be so rich,
I have a dream to play on a pitch.
I have a dream to do some skill,
I have a dream to take the test with no pill,
I have a dream to be the best,
I have a dream to beat the rest.
I have a dream to drive a car,
I have a dream to play midfield,
I have a dream to win the FA Cup,
I have a dream to be so famous.
I have a dream to play for Man U,
I have a dream to go through,
I have a dream to be a football player.

Mosa Jassim (13)
Priestnall School

I Have A Dream

Black and burning with poisonous smoke,
Engulfing shattered remains of buildings till they choke,
Barren wasteland looms across,
No people, no plants, no animals, it's all a loss.

Humans could have lived and humans could have thrived,
But power overtook them and eventually they died.
Karma was a belief that simply used to say,
Do something wrong and it will catch up with you one day.

It's sad for the world and I'm sorry to say
That they ignored Karma's gentle warning and carried on anyway.
The polar ice-caps melted, the ozone layer decreased,
Idiots put up more buildings, the environment was poor,
The abuse that they inflicted shook Earth to its core.

Humans were in anarchy, the government had lost control
And the price for their arrogance slowly took its toll.
But if we work harder, this morbid future can be changed,
Our world will be a paradise, not barbaric and deranged.

We all are individuals, we all can make a change,
One person can change the world, that thought isn't so strange.
I dream that our perfect world some day will come true,
But until it does, I'll write my poem to get my point across to you.

Sophie Dunne (13)
Priestnall School

Black Or White - Who Cares?

I have a dream to effect change.
Racism should stop, before it's too late.
Just because they're a different colour, it doesn't change.
We should do something about it, why wait?

What's the use in waiting?
People say they'll do it tomorrow, why not today?
We could at least try to stop the hating,
Then we can send the racist people on their way.

It isn't funny, big or clever,
Think how they must feel.
I believe we must stop it from now till ever
And let them have a chance to heal.

I don't see why they should be treated differently,
Just because of their skin.
It touches their hearts very gently,
You make it sound like a sin!

So I have a dream to effect change,
We can stop racism before it's too late.
They have a different skin colour, how does that change?
We can do something about it, so stop the wait!

Robyn Egan (13)
Priestnall School

I Have A Dream

I have a dream
That there is no war,
No famine,
No poor.

No more war,
No more planes,
No more shooting,
No more pain.

I have a dream of no famine,
Nobody would die,
No starving, there isn't enough food,
That is a lie.

There are no poor,
No boxes as homes for tramps,
Out in the cold,
Out in the damp.

James Smith (13)
Priestnall School

I Have A Dream

I had a dream about stopping all wars,
It scared, yet excited me, all at once.
No more bodies lying dead on the floor,
Now this is the army's last ever chance.
People living in peace and harmony,
No more fights and wars to disturb us now.
Instead of wars and fights we say sorry,
People say you can't stop wars. Can you? How?
War doesn't accomplish anything right,
It doesn't make anyone feel good.
So stop every war and stop all the fights,
Just stop them all now and make it right.

Lucy Anderson-Beswick (12)
Priestnall School

I Have A Dream

I had a dream
That there was no school,
Because all I do in English
Is snore and drool.
I'd go to the pub
And have a round of pool.
If only we didn't
Have to go to school.

I have a dream
To be a mouse
And wander around
From house to house,
To explore and see
The world at its best,
And hope not to be
Too big of a pest.

Jack McCreery (13)
Priestnall School

I Have A Dream

I dream of chocolate mountains tall,
And how I would eat them to make them small,
Of lying under a custard sun,
And dream of eating chocolate buns.

I dream of cars all made of jelly,
I watch them travel in a road of spaghetti.
They wibble and wobble until they stop,
With tyres of liquorice and candy drops.

I dream of all the food I like to eat
And stay here just to sleep and sleep.
Instead of eating food I enjoy,
My mum is there just to annoy,
With carrots and fruit and all things good,
A healthy diet for me - who would?

Catharine Bates (12)
Priestnall School

I Have A Dream

I used to know a child
Who used to cry all night,
Her father used to hurt her,
Her parents gave her a fright.

She woke up the next morning
Then it suddenly clicked,
She went for an audition,
Faith helped to be picked.

About ten years later,
Her life began to fall,
Her dad became very ill,
Her head against the wall.

Her baby was on the way,
Her career was in full whack,
The baby's father gave her drugs
So her head had no tap.

Two years later
She started to sing.
A man saw her
To see her thing.

All she wanted was a normal life,
Every Sunday she prays for Christ.
All the love in her heart
Tears her life miles apart!

Charlotte Ogden (13)
Priestnall School

I Have A Dream

Goal, goal, goal,
Three wonderful goals
In the back of the net.
The crowd go wild as
I score a hat-trick.
The great skill as
I go passed two more
Players I'm through
On goal, spinning the
Football into the
Top corner of the net.
I hold my breath,
The crowd go all quiet,
Could this be the
Winning goal,
With ten seconds to go?
The Champions League,
A second away.
Will we win or
Will we lose?
The clock ticks by,
A second to go,
The ball carries on
Spinning . . . *goal!*
I can't believe it,
I've scored,
But that's just my dream.

Tom Heppenstall (13)
Priestnall School

I Have A Dream

I have a dream . . .
That every time you switch on the TV
You are not begged by charities for money
And then they show starving children
With ribs and bones bursting out of skin.

I have a dream . . .
That gravestones didn't have to be built
Saying, 'To a soldier who lost his life'
Because they can't identify him
Because he's been blown to smithereens.

I have a dream . . .
That there are no wars where there are
Guns and bombs exploding every minute
And families sitting at home wondering
If they will be the next family in mourning.

I have a dream . . .
That you could go to a football match
Or walk down the street without
Having a racist stand and chant abuse at you,
Or being classed for your culture or your nature.

I have a dream . . .
That everyone cares for each other
So that we don't have to be persuaded by
Celebrities to help Third World countries,
Where some children don't have a mummy or daddy.

Sarah Bushell (12)
Priestnall School

I Have A Dream

My dream, my dream, my dream is so hollow,
Adulthood will come and wealth will follow.
Middle class citizenship though a thing that I hate,
With riches will soon become one of my traits.

I know I have low hopes,
I know it's pathetic,
I could do better - I'm quite well read,
But the smell of money is what gets me out of bed!

Winning the lottery, owning a business,
Whatever it is, however it is,
So long as I come out clean,
When I have a little, to get more I would be keen.

With money I could do as I wish,
I could change the rhyme pattern just like this!
But if I do, nobody will care,
I could also make up words to find a rhyme, like binaree.

I could get what I want
And not be branded 'spoilt',
My life as a rich man could be fab.
I would own a Ferrari - I wouldn't need to get a cab.

My dream, my dream, my dream is so hollow,
Adulthood will come and wealth will follow.
Middle class citizenship, though a thing that I hate,
With riches will soon become one of my traits.

Joseph White (12)
Priestnall School

I Have A Dream

I have a dream
That there is no school,
Because if there isn't,
That will be extremely cool.

The lessons are boring,
Especially science,
It is the worst subject ever,
And is a load of nonsense.

The school dinners are rubbish,
I eat them and I want to be sick.
If only we had lovely food
That doesn't taste of garlic!

I have a dream
That there is no school,
Because if there isn't,
That will be extremely cool.

Megan Whitehurst (13)
Priestnall School

I Have A Dream

What's the point of arguing?
What's the point of killing?
All it does is ruin our living.

Kill them with a gun,
Kill them with a knife,
Doesn't matter which, you shouldn't take his life.

The sound of a gun,
The body was lying,
Daughter and son by his side crying.

The blood of the body
Spilling across the dirty floor,
The moral of the story is to never start a war.

Aidan McGaughey (13)
Priestnall School

My Dream

I have a dream, do you have one too?
I love playing football, how about you?
I watch football of all levels
And different age groups too,
Especially the Premiership and Champions League,
So I can see what they can do.

Manchester United have the best players,
Although I support Manchester United,
I support County's progress as well,
Giggs, Rooney and Ronaldo are the best,
Mind you, so are the rest.

So as you can see, my dream is to be
A professional football player,
Playing for a Premiership club,
Ideally playing for Man Utd,
Winning lots of FA Cups.

Ryan Collett (13)
Priestnall School

Everywhere I Look Today

Everywhere I look today
I see hunger and suffering in every way.
Children crying
Cos they are dying.
Yes, people set up charity,
But that's only one step towards clarity.
So some people do try,
But that doesn't stop a cry,
A cry for help,
Cos people still die and yelp.
From the words of a legend,
'I have a dream'
For everyone to be equal
As a team.

Nick Baker (13)
Priestnall School

I Have A Dream

I have a dream
That racism will stop
No matter what colour you are
We're all the same

Black or white
Brown or pale
What difference does it make?
Because we're all the same

Colour doesn't matter
Neither does religion
Accept people for who they are
Accept for what they are not

Racism causes hate
Racism causes fights
Why not stop it
And give everyone their rights?

Racism is a big problem
It takes place everywhere
People get attacked
It's really not fair

Racism causes anguish
Racism causes pain
Think of other people's feelings
Stop this foolish game

I wish that racism will stop
So everyone will have some peace
So why doesn't it?
Just give people a chance at least

Don't look at their colour
Don't look at their race
Respect people for their culture
And respect them for their faith

Don't judge a book by its cover
Don't judge a person by the colour of their face
Love and respect one another
It doesn't matter whether one is from India, Jamaica or Spain

The world would be a better place
If there was no racism or hate
So think twice
Before you act
Stop racism!

Aroosa Choudhry (13)
Priestnall School

I Have A Dream

I have a dream,
A dream of a better place to live,
A dream of tranquillity,
A dream of peace,
A dream of colour and happiness.

I have a dream,
I want to help achieve,
I want to have,
I want to share,
I want to have everyone live there.

I have a dream,
I would love to do,
I would love to see,
I would love to experience,
I would love to be.

I have a dream,
It has to be real,
It has to come,
It has to happen,
It has to be done.

Lauren Hodgkinson (12)
Priestnall School

I Have A Dream

As everyone stood and stared,
No one really was prepared.
They watched the planes soar so high,
No one predicted that people would die.

It was horrible, blood everywhere,
It definitely came as a scare.
One plane, two planes, three planes, four,
An act like this still didn't stop the war.

He jumped out of the window, took his own life,
The pictures in the paper were shown to his wife.
'Pictures of the jump, what have you done?'
This is life or death, it's not for fun.

That terrorist, bin Laden, he likes to kill,
But we beat the war, overcame that hill
Where was God in their hour of need?
We worship Him and He can't do one deed.

Sam Rix (13)
Priestnall School

I Have A Dream For Racism To Stop

Racism happens all the time,
It hurts and it's a crime.
People who do it don't seem to care,
Is there any hope anywhere?

Racism happens everywhere,
You can't hide from it, it's always there.
What is the point?
What is the need?
It is worse than stealing and greed.

Why do people judge by the colour of your skin?
We're all the same on the outside and in.
It doesn't matter about religion and race,
In this world we all share a place.

Racism isn't big or great,
It only shows hurt and hate.
It's not only hurtful, it scars for life,
So before you do it, think twice.

Liliana McFadyen (13)
Priestnall School

I Have A Dream Of . . .

I have a dream that tomorrow will be sunny,
On Easter morning comes the chocolate bunny.

I have a dream that poverty could stop,
A helping hand could turn back the clock.

I have a dream that the world will be one,
So that all bad and evil will be gone.

I have a dream that everyone will be equal,
So that every person will become happy people.

I have a dream that friends will last,
So that every person will have a good past.

I have a dream that tomorrow will be sunny,
On Easter morning comes the chocolate bunny.

Lucy Nash (13)
Priestnall School

Racism And Poverty

Poverty is cruel, poverty isn't right,
Poverty doesn't get better at night.
Racism, cut us some slack, 'We are black.'
Racism, I've got the sack, *'I am black.'*
Poverty, Africa thinks it is 'tight',
Poverty, not enough food, don't fight.
Racism, roof's caved in, it had a crack,
Racism, can't get a job, black; don't mock
Poverty, can't get away, can't take a flight,
Poverty, countries near us might be all right.
When these merge together it is worse,
I hate this, it is not fair, follow the hearse.

Hasina Sattar (13)
Priestnall School

I Have A Dream . . .

I have a dream to help everyone who is poor
And give them all the money,
If this happens we can open a new door,
For the poor, for sure, this isn't funny.

There are people lying on the streets
In pain, dying, every day,
We should lend them a hand and pull them back on their feet,
If not now, we could pay.

Why are we leaving people on the streets in pain
And watching babies with no parents die?
If you were in their shoes, you would want everyone to feel your pain,
We should be ashamed and want to cry.

There are people in the world who just think of themselves
And all of what they've got,
So they should stop and take a look
At those less fortunate who are starting to rot.

Can we stop this madness
And stop all of the crying?
The world is full of sadness
Because the poor keep dying.

If everyone wrote a letter
To the leaders of the Earth,
Together we could make it better,
What would that be worth?

I have a dream to help everyone who is poor
And give them all money,
If this happens we can open a new door,
For the poor, for sure, this isn't funny.

Dominic Cook (13)
Priestnall School

I Have A Dream

I have a dream where I can fly,
Soaring through the sky up high.
Gliding and diving, enjoying the sights,
How little things look from such heights.

The clouds float by and offer me rest,
But I find the peace is the best.
My thoughts are empty, so I feel no stress,
I am just enjoying the peacefulness.

The birds flap their wings and come by my side,
They are not frightened, neither am I.

I feel so free, it's how I want to be,
I need to express my honesty.
Flying is fantastic, just close your eyes
And hopefully you'll feel just like me.

Jack O'Rourke (13)
Priestnall School

I Have A Dream!

I have a dream,
I dream of standing on stage,
The curtains opening,
The audience engaged,
I have a dream.

Singing like a nightingale,
Dancing to my hit,
I would love all the fame and fortune,
Oh, I would do anything for it.
I have a dream.

A dream is not something you live with,
It's something you can't live without.
My dream is what I'm living for,
My dream is who I am and what I'm all about!

Amy Bowden (13)
Priestnall School

I Have A Dream

How did we know
The wave was soon to come?
How did we know
We'd have to run?

No warning could save the people now,
Lots were swimming in the sea.
How could no one know this, how?
The end was soon to be.

People looked up, up to see
Their life to be washed away.
The victims thought, *how could this be,*
Our very last day?

The wave was finally here,
Right now it was ready to fall.
People looked away in fear,
They had no warning, nothing at all.

All thought it was their last to live,
Children, women and men,
They thought there'd be nothing else to give,
Even children younger than ten.

The tidal wave above their heads,
Can't believe what went wrong.
One last lie inside their beds,
Oh what took so long?

Finally the rescue team came,
All survivors safe now.
Who are we saying is to blame,
How could this happen, oh how?

My dream is for there to be no more of these
And people to send out warnings for when there is one.
This was the tsunami, a terrible day
That destroyed most of Indonesia and other places.

Samantha Lamerton (12)
Priestnall School

I Have A Dream

I have a dream
That our world is rid of poverty,
That no child is hungry,
Us all living equally.

I have a dream
That the colour of our skin doesn't matter,
Both black and white together,
Us all living equally.

I have a dream
That our world will be at peace,
No war, no fighting, no terrorism,
Us all living equally.

I have a dream
That no person will be looked down on,
No matter what they look like, no matter what religion,
Us all living equally.

Not just one dream, but many.

Yasmin Hasoon (12)
Priestnall School

I Once Had A Dream

I once had a dream
In world where it was so quiet and clean.
Animals running around
And plants growing from the ground.

I once had a dream
Where it was just me.
I walked around and explored the place,
Not knowing what I would face.

I'd never seen the sky so clear,
It felt like happiness was near.
Then I started walking on,
Wondering where everything had gone.

It started to get dark
And I got very scared.
I once had a dream,
But it wasn't as it seemed.

Was it all a dream?

Henna Bari (13)
Priestnall School

I Have A Dream

I have a dream that racism doesn't exist,
That when a black person is seen,
They won't be booed or hissed.

I have a dream whilst people who are rich,
Why are people in Africa
Drinking out of a ditch?

I have a dream that we can all get along
And share our money,
So come, world leaders, it isn't fair and it isn't funny.

I have a dream that poverty would just disappear,
So that the rest of the world
Wouldn't have to live in fear.

I have a dream that we all live in peace,
That all the bad people
Would be put on a leash.

I have a dream that there will never be a war,
That there is an *exit* sign
Above the door.

Will Bailey (12)
Priestnall School

Extraordinary

Life is extraordinary, it's a bad thing to waste,
But it's hard to stay alive with guns all over the place.

I know this because my grandma is dead,
That vicious disease took her in her bed.

Life is getting better, the bombs are put away,
London's tubes are safe now, they aren't getting blown away.

The war in Iraq is over, they are starting a new fresh life,
All the arguing is over, Saddam has said goodnight.

Dujon Lattie (13)
Priestnall School

Life Would Be Better . . .

Poor little Jess, being bullied at school,
She's small and fat, and isn't very cool.
Life would be better if she were left on her own,
Why won't they stop and just leave her alone?

Poor little Jess, tries to tell somebody,
They aren't really listening, just nod along like Noddy.
Life would be better if they stopped taking the mick,
Instead they carry on giving her leg a sly little kick.

Poor little Jess, getting hit in the playground,
She runs away and hides, not wanting to be found.
Life would be better if she went to a different school,
She'd be one of the cool kids, not the class fool.

Poor little Jess, they ripped up her work,
Then run up to their daddy in his brand new Merc.
Life would be better if her family was like that,
Instead she has to dress in second hand tat.

Poor little Jess, feeling sad and upset,
The bullies were laughing at her, shouting, 'teacher's pet'.
Life would be better if she could do whatever
She wanted to do, forever and ever.

Poor little Jess, can't even tell her own mum,
Because she gives her that stare, one which makes her feel numb.
Life would be better without all this hassle,
If she could live her dream to stay in a castle.

Poor little Jess, can't take it anymore,
Runs away from home, unhappy and poor.
Gets on the train, the train to Scotland,
Nobody there, no one to hold her hand.

Livie Kemp (13)
Priestnall School

The World We Live In

Crime, guns, fighting,
Death, murder, crying,
This poem that I'm writing
Is about people dying.

Druggies in the alleyways,
Scallies on the streets,
These are the days
When geeks get beat.

Gangs rule the ghetto,
All the cops are bent,
Thugs are robbing Netto,
And people won't pay their rent.

The world isn't dominated yet
By gangs and violent crime,
But if we let it, this is how it could get
And all it takes is time.

If we want a life
Which isn't lived in fear,
By a person with a knife,
Do something about it, the time is near.

James McCalla (13)
Priestnall School

This Is My Dream

While rich celebrities
Are in the fame,
People in Africa
Are going through pain.
We need to give them the money,
This is my dream,
So no need for greed.

If we buy new water wells
For the people who need it most,
We can change their lives
With a simple donation in the post.
We need to give them the fresh water that they need,
This is my dream,
So no need for greed.

So next time you're tucking into
Your favourite thing to eat,
Just remember to think about
The people living on the street.
We need to give them everything they need,
This is my dream,
So no need for greed.

Jack Oswald (13)
Priestnall School

Dreaming . . .

I have a dream,
A dream where generations ahead
Have better lives than ours.

I have a dream,
A dream where people will learn
That resources won't last forever.

I have a dream,
A dream where people live freely and
Are not cursed with the fear of bullies.

I have a dream,
A dream where people are treated
For their personality and not their appearance.

I have a dream,
A dream where countries will live as one
And be free from endless war.

I have a dream,
A dream where my words will be acknowledged
And my dreams will have come true.

I have a dream . . .

Hayley Lowe (13)
Priestnall School

Perfect World

Look outside, grey world you see . . .
Wars, hunger, pain, division, crime.
Think how you'd want it to be,
Think but take your time.
The perfect world . . .

Where people would cherish
Every single day,
Where no one's selfish
And we mean what we say.
The perfect world . . .

If I could help . . .
There would be no hunger,
No death,
No one feeling worse.
I wish I could change people.
The perfect world . . .

Imagine the world, totally new,
Where you could count on everyone
And everyone could count on you.
I wish it was like that,
The perfect world.

Blanka Kurp (13)
Priestnall School

Maradona

Diego Maradona, Diego Maradona,
He turns on the heat,
But he can be a cheat.
He still has magical feet.

Diego Maradona, Diego Maradona,
He scores a great goal,
He digs defenders into a hole,
But he still has a good soul.

Diego Maradona, Diego Maradona,
He may take drugs,
But he still isn't one of those mugs,
It just gets him away from the thugs.

Diego Maradona, Diego Maradona,
He can play as a striker,
Midfielder, but
Definitely not a defender.

Diego Maradona, Diego Maradona,
He plays in the light blue stripes,
You'd better believe the hypes,
There are not many of these types.

Diego Maradona, Diego Maradona,
He doesn't seem to try,
He still makes teams cry.
The legend of Maradona will never die.

Jack Howden (12)
Priestnall School

Bullies

It's not what is outside
Of the bully,
It's about what is inside
The bully.

It might have happened to them.
Inside they are hurting
As much as you.

Why do they do this?
Why do they hurt other people?
What has happened to them?

They do cry at night,
But look hard in the light.

Why do they do this?
Why do they hurt other people?
What has happened to them?

It's dark - bright is a fright.
It's light - the bully hurt me?

Why do they do this?
Why do they hurt other people?
What has happened to them?

Find the way,
Find the bullies
That bullied them.

Jake Carnie (13)
Priestnall School

Imagine The World Was In Your Hands

Imagine, imagine,
The world was
In your hands,
Tied to you by
Tiny wristbands.
The world was
Pretty light and
Looking very bright.

Imagine, imagine,
You could stop
War and make
A much better law,
And maybe even
Heal a dog's hurt paw.

Imagine, imagine,
You had a speech
As powerful as
Martin Luther King's
And people cherished it
As much as a
Big diamond ring,
And people don't
Just say that
Speech was bling bling,
Like they would
A flashy ring.

Imagine, imagine,
Your powerful thoughts
Were scattered in a river
And flowed into sea to sea
And people spotted
Them with glee.
They flowed from places,
To places and never
Tied in knots like
Big shoe laces.

Imagine, imagine
The world was in
Your hands as
It stands.
They say success comes
In cans and not in cannots.

Paige Rogers (12)
Priestnall School

Martin Luther King

Martin Luther King,
A black boy,
He did something
For the world
For all of the black people.
It's nice,
But sometimes
We get sad.
It's bad,
But Martin didn't get scared,
He said that the skin colour
Was not important.
What is important is that
People, whoever they are,
What colour skin they have,
Live happily.
We have to try
For people around us.
If they are sad,
Don't be scared,
Try helping them.

Hanieh Hazraty (12)
Priestnall School

Don't Judge By Looks

I have a dream . . .
That people will judge
By what one learns in books,
Instead of tormenting them for their looks.

I have a dream . . .
Why can't the people
With a misguided face
Join in with the human race?

I have a dream . . .
Why do they live in shame
Just because of how they look,
Why can't they share glory and fame?

I have a dream . . .
That one day you'll see
That they're no different
From you and me, so please just let them be.

So if you ever see someone
With problems you don't have,
And if you've lived a happy life,
Please do your best not to laugh.

Ryan Williams (12)
Priestnall School

Who Inspires Me . . .

The people that inspire me
Are very hard to choose,
So shut up, listen,
Then you will see . . .

First there is Hannan,
She's my best mate.
She is sassy and stylish
And always has a good-looking date.

Next there is Zanraa,
She's always there for me.
She has one main passion,
She has a passion for fashion.

Then there is Livie,
She's athletic and sporty,
She's very funny
And always there for me.

So they're the people
That inspire me.
Why not think of yours
And let your heart run free?

Megan Hughes (13)
Priestnall School

Martin Luther King

Martin wanted to dream,
The world to be one,
His family loved him
But then he was gone.

All he wanted was peace,
Some people agreed,
Some people disagreed,
One person took it to heart
And took him instead.

Martin loved his family,
Martin loved the world,
Martin didn't want to die,
But the end was here.

Martin's life was worthwhile,
He stood up and said his mind.
Don't be scared to say your mind too.

Tanzeela Mahboob (12)
Priestnall School

London

The London bombings,
A bus blown to death,
Some might have survived, but most died,
Nobody is trusted.

A bomb went off on a train,
People injured,
You could hear the screams,
Everybody in tears.

Nobody likes the terrorists,
They hate other countries.
People run in fear from them,
No one to help.

Everyone loved each other,
Even what happened here.
We should stay together,
No matter what the future brings.

Chelsea Lee (13)
Priestnall School

I Have A Dream . . .

As daylight fades and darkness falls,
My dreams start to call.
Thoughts flitter through my head,
As I lie on my bed.

My eyes start to close,
My thoughts become reality.
Seems like I'm living in a fantasy,
Where everything is desirable.

So much evil in the world,
Children crying, dying like ants in a stampede.
Having to do hard labour because of poverty and famine.
Is that right?

It needs to *stop* today.

So much evil in the world,
Where black and white people can't get along,
Just because of 'the colour of their skin, not the content of their heart',
Why is this?

It needs to *stop* today.

Why have we let the world get this bad?
Wouldn't it be nice if we could all live as one?
If we could 'love our neighbour as we love ourselves',
Why isn't it like this?

So much evil in the world.
This needs to stop today.

Katie Purlackee (12)
Priestnall School

If We Lived In Bliss

Every night when that child goes home,
They must feel like they are all alone.
Why should they be bullied for the colour of their skin?
Is this just the jealousy the others have within?
The world we live in is very mixed,
Why don't people just realise this?

Everyone is the same,
Just like you and me.
The pushing, shoving and names they call,
They shouldn't have to stand for it at all.

Why is the colour of their skin
So painful for others to bear?
Why can't we all be equal,
Where everyone can share?
The world we live in is very mixed,
Why don't people just realise this?

The colour of your skin
Does not mean anything.
So should we just accept it,
The racism in the world?
Sit around and do nothing,
Until someone makes themself heard!

Let's put all of our heads together
And find a solution for this,
Wouldn't the world be a happier place
If we all lived in bliss?

Sofia Dahou (12)
Priestnall School

Don't Judge Me If You Don't Know Me

People judge people by what they see,
Not by what they hear or what they've known.
Just take a second thought,
Have you ever been judged
By the look of your face,
Or the case that you face?

One day you'll find them nice and kind,
Didn't you just get that out of your mind?

So get to think before you judge anybody,
Because you might break somebody's heart
Inside their body.

Take a second chance with them,
To get to know them, before
You even get to throw them.

So it's time to make a change,
It's time to build anew,
Then there will be a day
When they'll not forget you.

Abdul Al Rebdi (12)
Priestnall School

The Pain Of Africa

Cracked lips, parched land,
Dusty promises of help at hand.
How can we make the love last?
How can we help a world that's growing too fast?

I wish it would rain on Africa,
Wash out the pain of Africa.

White clouds gathering would bring relief,
Lighter days with hope and peace.
Bush won't cancel Africa's debts,
We can't imagine the pain they've met.

I wish it would rain on Africa,
Wash out the pain of Africa.

Guns and bombs, tears and mud,
Long white limos, race through blood,
But bound by debt to hopelessness,
Can we ever clean this mess?

Wash out the pain of Africa.

Freya Ernstbrunner (12)
Priestnall School

I Have A Dream

I have a dream that we'll all live side by side,
With everyone in perfect harmony
And everyone would rather have love
Than medals won at any ceremony.

I have a dream that racism will end,
And the world will be completely tolerant
Of others' religion and their lifestyle
And war will be something no one will want.

I have a dream that there will be no poverty
And no one will die of starvation,
Or die of a petty illness
Cos they can't afford the medication.

I have a dream that there will be no fighting
And someone will put an end to violence,
And the only thing we'll go to see at the cinema
Will be something that contains romance.

Alex Hardy (12)
Priestnall School

My Dream

When people are starving and being gloomy
And others are happy and very wealthy,
It is stupid when you can't spare some money
For the poor people who don't find it funny.
Why can't poverty be gone
And there will be food for everyone?
It's so unfair when you stuff your face,
When you're not hungry and don't take your pace.
I have a dream
And I want it to be seen.

Geraldine McIntyre (13)
Priestnall School

George Bush Lying, People Dying

Religion's the cause of many wars,
You know you can't stop it.
I wish all people would accept beliefs
Or just ignore them and drop it.

Because of racism
Right now kids are dying,
All because of stupid reasons,
Like George Bush's constant lying.

Religion has unfortunately caused
Troops to go to Baghdad.
They haven't come home yet,
George Bush must be mad.

Bush says he stands for equal rights,
He says he is no racist,
But where black people live
Are liquor stores and gun places.

Will Jenkinson-Druck (13)
Priestnall School

Six Billion

With over six billion people in the world
It's hard to choose one person who inspires you.
With over six billion opinions in the world
It's hard to choose one you really agree with.
With over six billion people with talents,
It's hard to believe you are unique.
But when one person inspires you
Through music, or art, or drama,
You can really look up to them,
And it doesn't matter if no one else likes them,
Because if just one person looks up to them,
It doesn't matter about the other six billion.

Eleanor Haynes (12)
Priestnall School

A World Without Terrorism

My opinion on terrorism
Is really quite plain,
Terrorism is evil and
Causes lots of pain.

Lots of countries suffer this pain,
Sri Lanka and Iraq,
Congo and Afghanistan,
The terrorists keep coming back.

A world without terrorism,
What a world that would be!
Everybody is joyous
In each and every country.

My idea is *stop terrorism*
And I think some people might agree,
To stop all this revulsion
And leave the countries be.

Amy Johnson (12)
Priestnall School

Racism

At the moment in the world all is not well,
Some stupid people put others through hell.
The colour of people's skin doesn't matter,
Racism just makes people's lives shatter.

Everybody is the same,
Ignoring that is just lame.
If you're prejudiced against people's skin colour,
Well, if you think a dog is dumb, you're much dumber.

Whether you're white, black, brown, or even green,
Being racist is just mean.
Nobody's skin colour is exactly the same,
Teasing people for this just isn't a game.

Without racism the world would be great,
There would be a lot less hate.
So I tell you racism is very bad,
Committing it yourself is just mad.

Joe Horsman (12)
Priestnall School

My View On The World

My view on the world
Is that it should change
And those who stop it
Should end up in chains.

We start off with bullying,
Which should be first to stop,
And those who do it
Should be left to rot.

Next up is racism,
Which is the worst of the lot,
And we should all get together
To get it to stop.

We move on to terrorism,
A terrible crime,
But we must give people hell
To get off that line.

Moving on to war,
Being more frequently used
By the world's greatest leaders
Who, more often that not, lose!

We need a better world,
One for people to live in.
We need a better world,
Preferably one with less sin.

So finally in conclusion,
We know we need to improve,
But as for how to do this,
We have something to prove.

Ian McGuinness (13)
Priestnall School

World In A Washing Machine

I would like to take the world in hand,
Put it in a washing machine,
Get rid of all the bad things
And bring it out perfect and clean.

I would like to pick up racism
And bundle it into a sack,
Tie the knot and throw it
So it's lost and can't come back.

I would like to rent a boat,
Get bullying up on deck,
Then plummet to the ocean floor,
Make sure it's gone, I'll check.

I would like to call up poverty,
Make it line up, I'll light the flame
And burn it on a bonfire,
Never to be seen again.

I would like to collect up all abuse
And stop it feeling clever,
I'd build a wall around it,
It would be trapped forever.

I would like to find all war and lead it
To a house away from you and me,
Lock the doors and windows,
Then throw away the key.

I would like to take the world in hand,
Put it in a washing machine,
Get rid of all the bad things
And bring it out perfect and clean.

Sarah Taylor (13)
Priestnall School

I Have A Dream

I have a dream that animals will be protected
And all the poor people won't be rejected.
I want world poverty to be gone
And there to be food and water for everyone.

I have a dream that there will be no more school,
Then all the kids will think the world will be cool.
Everyone should be treated as one,
And I want all evil to be gone.

I have a dream that it will be sunny,
For Easter I want a big chocolate bunny.
I want global warning to come to an end
So Mother Earth can be on the mend.

I have a dream that the world will be clean.
I want people to no longer be mean.
I want there to be no more war
And all sick people to find a cure.

Jasmine Gabbidon (12)
Priestnall School

I Have A Dream!

I have a dream everyone knows my name,
The lights shining on me.
I'm dancing in front of millions, it's not just a game.
People staring and clapping for me!

I have a dream, it's real life
And is not just for one night.
I have no worries, this is my life,
The smile glistens on my face as I end my dance.

I have a dream, as the curtains close I bow down,
The crowd goes wild, people jumping up and down.
I go home proud,
People still talking about me.

I have a dream,
It isn't just any,
It's what I live for, my ambition.
I have a dream!

Robyn Dee (13)
Priestnall School

I Have A Dream

Last night as I lay asleep in bed,
I had a dream,
An interesting dream,
A dream that must be said.

There was no racism and no war,
There was no death and no poor,
Young helped old,
But without being told.

But when I open my eyes, I see a different story,
People kill people without glory.
People are raped, stabbed and shot,
Babies are snatched as they sleep in their cot.

Imagine all this could end,
Tragedy stops as you turn the next bend.
People replace all hate with love,
God looks down and smiles from above.

All this would stop, if we try hard.
Neighbours that hate you might send you a card.
Less people would be arrested and jailed by the law,
Without death, population would soar.

I'll tell you again what I've already said,
I had a dream,
An interesting dream,
A dream that must be said.

Thomas Brimage (12)
Priestnall School

I Have A Dream

I have a dream
To be able to draw,
To draw portraits
And colour them too!

To be able to dance
And enter competitions
To win them and be proud
Of my achievements.

To act on stage
And not be afraid
To get a leading role
And to be confident.

To swim out into the sea,
That will be amazing,
For me to swim far out
Away from the land.

To be able to run
Like in the Olympics,
To win a race and be happy
And to raise money for charity.

My dreams, my wishes, my hopes for the future,
Made by my heart and with me for life.

Elizabeth Whittaker (12)
Priestnall School

I Have A Dream

I have a dream to swim in the sea,
To have all kinds of fishes around me.
This blue planet has no sky,
A place, a land, where mussels lie.

Chat with dolphins, laugh and play,
Dance with rays that sing and sway.
Seaweed rustles beneath the waves,
Swimming deeper in the caves.

A mermaid's purse would make my day,
A mermaid's song I'd have to play.
If I could, I'd stay all day
And paint the clownfish on their way.

Shipwrecks loom out of the dark,
Be on your guard, watch out for sharks.
Electric eels may light your way,
Just make sure you're not their prey!

Crabs may bite and nip your toe,
There's just one thing you ought to know.
You may think you're big, you're not at all,
Compared to a whale, you're very small!

Jessica Walton (13)
Priestnall School

A Perfect World

I'm going to make a perfect world,
A world I'd like to see,
No more hunger,
War or suffering,
A world of harmony.

The field mice settle in the hedgerow,
The fish settle in the sea,
People all shake hands
And for once they all agree.

I'm going to make a perfect world,
Where anyone can live,
And if anyone does something wrong,
People will forgive.

No terrorism will be done,
No racism or discrimination to the world will come,
No people will cry in pain,
No people will cry because of evil names,
No people will be bullied,
No people will be worried,
Everyone will live in peace and harmony.

George Shore (13)
Priestnall School

I Have A Dream

Kirsty with the back-to-front heart
Really plays an inspiring part,
As she's only young
And has been through a lot,
You need determination and commitment
To handle what she's got.

She has her own charity
To help Francis House
For people like her
To make their lives better.
Celebs help Kirsty raise the money,
Like Posh and Becks who donate regularly.

She has been on the telly
To get her point across,
Showing the stubborn ones who is boss.
Remember to always hold your head high,
Words can't hurt you,
No need to cry.

It's hard to think about what she's been through,
Some people haven't heard of her, they don't have a clue,
But to me she's an inspiration
To what we can do,
And that's the main thing,
Hope you think that too.

Louise Hamilton (13)
Priestnall School

Dreams . . .

I have a dream that this world will be equal,
Just like people have tried to.
I have a dream that this world won't be dull
And everyone will do what they have to.

I have a dream just like everyone,
Martin Luther King and Nelson Mandela did as well.
They tried to restore the damage people have done,
I have a dream that I would like to tell.

They had a dream they all won,
Nelson Mandela won the Nobel Peace Prize.
I have a dream that we will all be one,
They saw a dream, they saw through their eyes.

Nelson had a dream to be free from jail,
His dream came true years after.
Now he is famous for his tale,
His dream happened years after.

I have a dream just like you,
To be free from the fighting and the law.
I have a dream that we could make a difference,
I have a dream to stop these wars.

Everyone has dreams, good or bad,
I have dreams and wishes too.
Everyone has dreams, happy or sad.
I have dreams, do you?

Alaina Chaudhry (12)
Priestnall School

My Dream

My dream is to live in a world
Where people aren't judged by their skin,
But are all treated equally
And by their character within.

And to live in a world
Where people aren't forced away
And treated differently.
But are welcomed to stay.

And to live in a world
Where people don't die
From guns firing bullets,
Which look like rain from the sky.

And to live in a world
Where people could see
How much damage and upset is caused,
And then live happily.

Sarah Bousfield (13)
Priestnall School

I Have A Dream!

I have a dream to stop war,
To make it against the law.
No more M5s,
Or any sharp knives!

No more machine guns
And no more deaths of parents' sons.
No more grenades
Or any other shiny blades!

Let's destroy every tank,
Make sure every submarine has sank.
This is my dream,
I hope it comes true!

Tom Fleetwood (13)
Priestnall School

I Have A Dream

I have a dream,
The icon standing clear and proud,
Changing people all around,
Their roots placed firmly on the ground.

I have a dream,
Great teacher teaching all they know,
All they know, now I, too, know.
They reveal all, I gasp, I know.

I have a dream,
I listen well, they still do tell,
I understand, I take it in,
I understand, now I go tell.

I have a dream,
Inspiration flowing through,
I take it in, I know it too,
They taught me well, now I know too.

I have a dream.

Adam Corbridge (13)
Priestnall School

If I Could Change The World, I Would

If I could change the world, I would,
Make people behave the way they should.
No fighting, poverty or war,
Like there's always been before.
People will respect others,
Treat everyone like sisters and brothers.
No murder, racism or discrimination,
We'll work together as a nation.
No more sadness, no more crying,
Stop the innocent from dying.
I want the world to be a better place,
We'll be together, every race.

Leah Spinoza & Florence Van Bergan (12)
Priestnall School

Change The World

Change the world,
Come with me,
Try to let your dreams fly free
And you know
It'll come so easily
In life.

Every moment
We're alive,
It's our love
That will survive,
Together we'll change the world.

There would be no poverty,
No diseases flying free.
Do you know
How easy it would be
If we tried?

We could make the perfect world,
No more gangs or wars.
Do you know how many people
Would feel reassured
In life?

Zahraa Alam-Cheetham (13)
Priestnall School

I Have A Dream

I dream I see a world with no war.
I have a dream,
Everyone in Africa is poor,
Everything must change.

Everywhere else, crime is high,
People all suffer more than needed.
At the rate we're going, the end is nigh,
All over the world bad things happen.

Child cruelty happens everywhere,
Things like this deserve to stop.
Children's minds and lives are not war and fear,
Always the children come second.

Everywhere I look there is suffering and pain,
Six billion people, all as guilty as the next,
No one thinks helping people has a gain,
I have a dream.

Everywhere there is a high rate of murder,
This can be stopped,
Criminals don't need to be pushed any further,
They need to be stopped.

Jonathan Garner (12)
Priestnall School

Together We Make A Rainbow

This world is far from perfect,
But I still have a dream
Of a world without racism
As there is too much of it, it seems.

As I look out of windows,
I notice both black and white.
Together we make a rainbow,
So why do people think colour isn't right?

Skin is just a covering,
It's what's underneath that counts,
Yet others can't see this way,
So racial tension mounts.

Bullying and murders,
Not accepting skin,
Join together to be united as one
Against this unfair sin.

But just how must those victims feel
Through each and every day
As they get bullied, oh so badly,
In each and every way.

The victims put on a brave face
Trying to forget the jeers,
But if we looked inside at the deep down feelings,
They'd be overwhelmed with tears.

If you can't accept a different race,
If you're really that unkind,
If you can't accept a different colour,
Then you might as well be blind.

Natalie Holt (13)
Priestnall School

I Have A Dream

I have a dream of fame and glory,
To act and dance and sing,
But my dream is just a story,
It will never mean anything.

I have a dram to be in the spotlight,
To be adored by billions.
I would be the star of the night,
My copies would sell millions.

I have a dream to be offered a job,
So I can act and dance and sing,
Then I wouldn't have to rob
And I could buy almost anything.

I have a dream to buy food for my wife
And my four children too,
Then they'd have a good life
And we could live in a house like you.

I have a dream to step out of the gutter
To enter this beautiful town,
Get away from the rats that scatter
And never see my children frown.

I have a dream to die without pain,
But I think to myself, no,
I'd have to tell my little son Shayne
That Daddy has to go.

I have a dream to die with a meaning,
Then my family can buy a house.
I can now hear people screaming,
As I fall from a sixty-foot house.

I had a dream to die for my loved ones
And now that dream's come true.

Ellie Rogers (13)
Priestnall School

I Have A Dream

Beverly Hills, that's where I want to be,
Livin' in Beverly Hills by the sea.

Look at all those movie stars,
They're all so beautiful and tall,
Their housemaids scrub the floors,
They get the spaces in the hall.

Beverly Hills, that's where I want to be,
Livin' in Beverly Hills by the sea.

I wanna live a lot like that,
I wanna be just like a king,
Take my picture by the pool
'Cause I'm the next big thing.

Beverly Hills, that's where I want to be,
Livin' in Beverly Hills by the sea

Where the pop stars scream and shout
And the cameras go *click, click, click.*
The models walk down the catwalk,
The jealous people just take the mick.

Beverly Hills, that's where I want to be,
Livin' in Beverly Hills by the sea.

Helen Thomas (13)
Priestnall School

I Dream

Oh I wish there was no war
And everybody wasn't poor.

Oh I wish everyone could see
And everyone living happily.

Poverty is such a horrid thing,
I wish everyone could just grow wings
And fly away from all the war,
Which is sometimes blamed on the poor.

Oh I wish there was no war
And everybody wasn't poor.

Oh I wish everyone could see
And everyone living happily.

For people to love and people to care
And if someone looks different we won't stare,
For it is rude and very unkind
And some people do mind.

Oh I wish there was no war
And everybody wasn't poor.

Oh I wish everyone could see
And everyone living happily.

Georgia Walkden (13)
Priestnall School

I Have A Dream!

I have a dream
Of stopping all wars,
To stop the fighting,
To open a door.

I have a dream
Of no more killing,
To help the world
With emptiness filling.

I have a dream
Of helping the needy,
To stop humanity
Being so greedy.

I have a dream
Of destroying all weapons,
To teach the people
A useful lesson.

I have a dream,
I hope it comes true,
I have a dream,
What about you?

Olivia Cork (12)
Priestnall School

I Have A Dream

This man had a dream of an easier world,
The man who brightened up our lives,
If he hadn't found it, we would live in turmoil,
And his discovery still survives.

If it were not for him, we would be using fire,
At night everyone would lose their way,
For his mark in history,
It will be bright and not grey.

His discovery led others to new inventions,
Without him we would not have cars,
What would we be without machines?
Life would truly be like living on Mars.

Thanks to him we live in an age
Where life is easy and not hard.
People forget what he did for us,
We should give him our regards.

For this person I look up to,
Many may not remember,
His name is Benjamin Franklin,
He gave us light in December.

Matthew Powell (13)
Priestnall School

Politics

('Our enemies are innovative and resourceful, and so are we. They never stop thinking about new ways to harm our country and neither do we'. George Bush, Washington DC, August 5th 2004)

They wear suits and drive expensive cars,
They drink champagne in fancy bars,
They think they're good, but they start wars,
They think and pass unfair laws.

They say they'll end all poverty,
But to that there is no guarantee,
They promise money they cannot pay,
When they'll give, they do not say.

They say they stand for racial equality,
But they will never ever see
That to stop racists, to stop the hate,
We need action before it's too late.

People like George Bush and Tony Blair,
They love money and do not care
If people die or are pelted with bricks,
They are our MPs, this is politics.

Robin Masters (13)
Priestnall School

I Have A Dream

I have a dream that minds would think alike,
I have a dream that people would stand up and fight,
I have a dream of clear blue skies,
I have a dream of truth and no lies,
I have a dream of poverty no more,
I have a dream of an open door,
I have a dream of no suffering and no pain,
I have a dream that people's rights were the same,
I have a dream I could get up and speak,
I have a dream there would be world peace.

Yan Trinh (13)
Priestnall School

It's A Multicoloured World!

Have you ever noticed
Those people in the street,
The way they walk, the way they talk,
The way they drag their feet?

Do you know those people,
Have you met before?
If not why bully them?
What reason for this coloured war?

A little girl is crying,
For she was bullied today.
Her chocolate skin so pretty,
She cries to take the pain away.

Is it simply jealousy
Or is it just plain spite?
Is it funny, just a game
To put this girl in fright?

At night that child goes home.
They toss and turn, they cannot sleep,
In depression and fear
Of tomorrow and what horror they will meet.

That horror's just a girl,
A tall and pale girl too,
But she can cause destruction
To her, or him, or you.

What if all could see this?
Would we change at all?
To see it only takes one girl
To cause another one to fall.

So next time you notice those people in the street,
Don't bully them, accept them, help them pick up their feet.

Polly Maxwell (12)
Priestnall School

I Have A Dream

A world of peace, of fun and glee,
No wars, no fights, no jealousy.

To paint and colour,
To sketch and draw,
This is my dream,
Pencils galore.

Still life paintings,
Pictures of the sea,
My ambition is my future,
Like my character and personality.

I want to paint the country,
I want to sketch the trees,
I'd like to draw the scenery,
I'll colour for you and me.

Sunny weather,
Summer to fall,
Spring showers,
I'll draw them all.

Get out your pencils,
Draw and you will see
Painting pictures is fun,
An artist is what I want to be.

Matthew Bennett (12)
Priestnall School

I Have A Dream

I have a dream
Capitalists have more money than the poor.
I have a dream
Poor people don't have enough sterilised water.
I have a dream
Poor people can't grow enough crops.
I have a dream
Poor people can't have a good wash.
I have a dream
Poor people don't have a good curriculum.
I have a dream
Poor people die of famine.
I have a dream
Poor people suffer in silence.
I have a dream
Poor people are in debt to the government.
I have a dream
Poor people don't have enough finances to buy clothes.
I have a dream
Poor people don't have doctors so they get very ill.
I have a dream
Poor people get infections very easily.
Let's not dream, let's put a stop to *poverty!*

Laura Rogers (12)
Priestnall School

I Have A Dream

Last night I had a dream
The world was falling apart at the seams.
There was war, poverty and disaster,
Killing people faster and faster.
There were earthquakes, fire and flood,
Swords, guns, bombs and blood.
I woke up and cried
For all the people who died.
I wish I could make the world a better place,
Somewhere we'd be happy to face.

I've never understood the way
People run the world each day.
Everyone thinks of themselves only,
One thought in their minds, just *me, me, me.*
What is all this hunger and greed
When there are so many people to feed?
Ignoring the people who knock on the door
Asking for money, for the disabled, for the poor.
I wish I could make people care,
Make them realise there are other people there.

Maybe this world is doomed to be
A place where people are unhappy,
A place with so much war and so many fights,
Is it just me, or is something not right?
People raise money for charity,
Why don't they understand, why don't they see
That there should be no need for this?
There's enough in the world to keep us all at peace.
I wish I could make people understand,
Make them live side by side, hand in hand.

Hatice Torun (12)
Priestnall School

A New Realm

We will create a realm of our own,
A place without many problems,
An Eden, a new universe, our home.

As we get stuck into our meals,
Do we ever stop to think
How an empty stomach feels?

In our beds we are curled,
Let us thank
That we are not of the Third World.

God had a place to lend,
We ruined it.
Pollution should not be the end.

What have we done?
We have caused too much chaos.
How did we get so dumb?

There is no one else but the Devil and ourselves to blame.
What is wrong with different coloured people?
Everybody should be treated the same.

If we all spoke white,
Our world would be like a blank page.
That wouldn't be a very nice sight.

The further we go, the dimmer it gets,
As we walk towards the end of the tunnel,
So a new target we must set.

Actions speak louder than words,
This is our world to keep.
Sometimes we must do rather than be heard.

We complain about a lot of things,
So let's do something about it.
Join in and sing.

Mai Vi Giang (13)
Priestnall School

Try To Smile!

I have dreams,
They'll make you smile.
I have dreams,
They'll make you frown.
I have dreams,
They'll make you laugh.
I have dreams,
They'll make you cry.

Many dreams are really something great.
They feel like they're never going to end.
Some dreams are awful,
So these feel like nightmares.

Everyone has someone they love,
But may sometimes wish they're gone.
But if they're gone,
How will you cope?

No one to argue with,
No one to shout at,
No one to call names.
That would be a nightmare.

But I have a dream
That's sure to bring a smile to your face.
I dream that there are no wars,
No fights, just love.
Dream that you'll live forever,
Just don't waste what you've got.

Kerry Laffey (12)
Priestnall School

I Have A Dream

I have a dream
Of this world as one,
A dream
Of black and white hand in hand.

But this is reality,
War and hate raging through this land,
People forgetting who they are
And what they could actually be.

But one man stood up,
With courage and determination,
A nation corrupted through power,
To unite this broken nation.

He did not break, he did not fall,
Pain and hate was in his path.
He walked right through them,
No cry, no laugh.

This one man succeeded,
The power he had was great,
He did not want power,
He did not even want fame.

He was not corrupted with power,
He was not bribed with money,
I have a dream in this world
To be like this person,

To help my country
And our world.

Ruari Spence (12)
Priestnall School

I Have A Dream

I pick the book off the shelf
And as I read, visions of colour and greatness
Come to me as no other book has.
I sit on the dusty floor and immerse myself.
The unique story surrounds me and I feel as the characters do.
As I come to the end, I sigh,
Yet it is a sigh of happiness
As I know that I shall never read such a book again.
I close the book and before I place it back upon the shelf,
I see its name for the first time,
'The Fire Within' by Chris d'Lacey,
And I know that I have been,
Inspired.

Davey Blackstock (12)
Priestnall School

I Have A Dream

I have a dream
That there will be no more negative attitudes.
I have a dream
That selfishness won't stand in the way of people's dreams.
I have a dream
That other people's power won't stand in the way of your goals.
I have a dream
That family and relationships won't stop people from pursuing their dreams,
Like a barrier has been put up around you.
I have a dream
That money won't stop you from achieving your goals.
I have a dream
That one day people will be able to carry out their dreams.
I have a dream!

Bryony Martin (12)
Priestnall School

Poor People Poem

Why do rich people always ignore the poor?
Why can't people help just that little bit more?
Poor people need education just as we do.
Water in their country can make them ill,
Even worse, it can kill!
Rich people think they are better than poor,
They have money and can afford things
And rate the poor people as not anything.
They need a place to live, a world to see,
But they suffer in poverty.
This is the end of my rich/poor rhyme,
We need your help, there's little time.
There is only a little time, so let's get it right.

Helen Stansfield-Boys (12)
Priestnall School

I Have A Dream

Rich people aren't bothered about the poor,
They spend their money on useless things,
They are very, very selfish!
They won't even send any money to the poor
So they're able to live longer.
The poor need the money more than the rich.
Imagine the poor drinking dirty water,
Imagine a child dying every three seconds.
There are not enough jobs for everyone.
Government aren't doing much about it.
Rich people take money for granted.
Poor children and adults have to live with dirty water
And aren't rich enough to buy clothes for themselves.
Not giving money is like having nothing.
Imagine poor people in starvation,
Imagine poor people dying.
It's just so unfair!
I have a dream that ends poverty now.

Laura Clayton (12)
Priestnall School

I Have A Dream

I have a dream
That the poor could afford warm clothes.
I have a dream
That the rich would give money to the poor.
I have a dream
That the poor were healthy.
I have a dream
That the rich would pay off their debts.
I have a dream
That the poor didn't have to beg like tramps.
I have a dream
That the poor had nice houses.
I have a dream
That the poor had lots and lots of money.
I have a dream
That the poor could live normal lives.
I have a dream
That the poor have clean water to wash with.
I have a dream.

Jack Aspinall (13)
Priestnall School

Racism

I don't get racism,
I just don't understand
Why people look at the colour
And not the woman or man.
If people got to know the person,
They would see that they were wrong.
Stop looking at them like animals
And then different people can get along.
Everyone's different,
No one's the same,
Let's stop racism
And make a change!

Natalie Walton (13)
Priestnall School

I Have A Dream!

I have a dream
That wars will stop.
I have a dream
That people will stop killing each other.
I have a dream
That someone will say there is no point in them.
I have a dream
That people will stop hurting others who haven't done
anything wrong.
I have a dream
That the sounds *bang, bang, bang,* will stop.
I have a dream.

Tom Grice (13)
Priestnall School

George Best

G oals, goals, goals
E nergetic
O ld Trafford
R IP, a legend
G eorgie, Georgie, they called him, a Belfast boy!
E ven better than Pele

B eautiful game
E ntire magic
S tamina, speed
T he best.

Ben Heron (13)
Priestnall School

I Have A Dream

I have a dream that I could
Live in my own fashion world . . .
What is fashion?
What is popular at the time
With style in the fashion line.
Doesn't matter your shape or size,
It is always nice to wear designs!
Hair and clothes make you shine,
So go and pick from our friendly lines!
Pinks, yellows, orange and green,
Pick a colour, I'm sure you'll scream!
Colours come alive so we can disguise
How we choose to pick from trendy lines!
Checks, squares, flowers and stripes,
Some look out of sight.
Modern or dated, I'm sure you'll choose
What really does suit you.
Fashion is like a flowing, textured
Stream of life!
Some even look nice.
Delightful shades of every hue,
There is sure to be something to suit you!

Lorna O'Rourke (13)
Priestnall School

I Have A Dream

I have a dream to watch Manchester United in a final,
I have a dream to listen to the stadium roar,
I have a dream to hear the drums going *boom, boom, boom,*
I have a dream to go to Wembley and support my team all the way,
I have a dream to run on the pitch when we have won a game,
I have a dream that I would be able to speak to the players
And hold the trophy and be proud of my team.

Tom Russell (12)
Priestnall School

Friendship

Friends are what people need,
Some people whine and plead,
Reliability is what friends are
And if you succeed, you will go far.
If you have no friends, it will bring sadness,
But if you have many, it will bring happiness.
We need friends, me and you,
And one day it will come true.
You and your friends playing every day,
Just imagine it's a summer's day.
Friends are always very loyal,
They make you feel all posh and royal.
Friends are very faithful
And then you are all so graceful.
That's what friends are all about.

Alex Murphy (13)
Priestnall School

I Have A Dream

I have a dream that one day we will be together,
All united as one,
With love and laughter
And with fun and friends.
I have a dream that one day
We will be together,
Where racism is unheard of
And hunger is no more.
I have a dream that one day we'll be together,
With no wars in the world
And the world for once in perfect harmony.
I have a dream that one day
We will all be united as one.
If I dream hard enough then maybe
The dream that I'm having
Will come true.

Polly Swindail (13)
Ruskin Sports College

I Have A Dream

I have a dream,
Of a world with no poverty.
I have a dream,
Where peace is all we see.

I have a dream,
Where we are all friends.
I have a dream,
Where bad things can mend.

I have a dream,
Where there is no racism.
I have a dream,
Where there is no prison.

I have a dream,
Where everyone cares.
I have a dream,
Where we can all share.

I have a dream,
Of peace and love.
Where Heaven doesn't just
Come from above.

That is my dream,
Our dream.

Jasmin Mosley (13)
Ruskin Sports College

Team World

I have a dream
To see a team
With black and white,
We have a right.

A dream have I
We can all bake pie,
All of us together,
For ever and ever.

I have a dream,
No kings or queens,
No countries or faiths,
No one to discriminate.

A dream have I,
No dodgy chavs,
No robbing or stealing,
It's all appealing.

Justice and freedom
For the United Kingdom,
To share our wealth
And improve Africa's health.

Maybe one day
My dream will pay,
The world will unite
And win the fight.

Liam Astley (13)
Ruskin Sports College

We Are One

I have a dream
To see a team
With black and white,
We all have equal rights.

A dream have I,
Can't we all try
To live together
Forever and ever?

I have a dream
There are no kings or queens,
No countries or faiths,
No one to discriminate.

Justice and freedom
For the United Kingdom,
No popularity,
No Third World countries in poverty.

So let's join hands
All over these lands.
Great minds think alike,
But great people's hearts beat as *one!*

Ryan Jones (12)
Ruskin Sports College

I Dream

I dream of a world
Without poverty or war,
A place to live my life
Without breaking the law.

I dream of a world
Where everyone cares,
People are happy
And everyone shares.

I dream of a world
Where everyone has the right
To a normal life,
Whether they're black or white.

I dream of a world
Where there is no famine,
And people are not judged
By the colour of their skin.

I dream of this world,
But no one will try
To help those who suffer
And those that die!

Emma Oakes (12)
Ruskin Sports College

I Have A Dream . . .

I have a dream,
A dream full of peace and love,
That Heaven was on Earth
And not just above.

I have a dream,
A dream full of freedom and imagination,
That everyone was happy,
We were one as a nation.

I have a dream,
A dream without racism and war,
A perfect world
Where no one is poor.

I have a dream,
A dream where everyone cares,
The people are joyous,
Everyone shares.

Sophie Cope (13)
Ruskin Sports College

I Have A Dream

The world will live in peace,
Everyone will be happy,
We will live together, in harmony,
This is my dream.
We can walk out in safety, be with any race,
We will not turn a blind eye,
This is my dream.
Education will be for everyone,
Freedom will bring us together,
We will be united as one,
We will understand other cultures.
This is my dream.

Sally Lewis (13)
Ruskin Sports College

I Have A Dream

I have a dream
That the world will live in peace,
Everyone will work in unison,
People throughout the world will be respected.

I have a dream
That all races will come together,
Sharing will become a way of life,
People throughout the world will be respected.

I have a dream
There are no possessions,
People will be free,
People throughout the world will be respected.

I have a dream
There will be no violence,
Things will be settled in a non-violent way,
People throughout the world will respect each other.

Jasmin Bromage (12)
Ruskin Sports College

I Have A Dream

I have a dream of no creed, no greed and no evil
Ripping at the seams. These are my best dreams.

Racist people and prejudiced people,
All are sick in the head.
They can throw criticisms
And make jokes,
But at the end of the day,
The joke's on them
And their sad lives.
I have a dream
That one day this will stop
And it will come to an end,
Making racism history.

Matthew Readdin (12)
Ruskin Sports College

I Dream Of A World

I dream of a world
Without poverty or war,
Where no one breaks promises
And no one breaks the laws.

I dream of a world
Where there's no famine or fights,
Where nobody argues
Over legal rights.

I dream of a world
Where no racism exists,
But kindness and happiness
Still persists.

I dream of a world
Where we will all share,
If we all work together,
No plates will be bare.

I dream of a world
Without suffering and dying,
People alone and
People that are crying.

I dream of this world
But it will have to be fought,
As no one will listen,
Unless it is bought.

Emily Hatton (12)
Ruskin Sports College

I Have A Dream

I have a dream
That no one in Africa
Will die of starvation,
And nobody else
Through the nation.

I have a dream
That no one will
Have any possessions,
Then all as one
We will have many possessions.

I have a dream
That there will be no war,
No fighting and no killing,
And plenty of money
For the poor.

I have a dream
That racism is abolished,
No violence and no bias
And everywhere
Will be polished.

I have a dream
That there will be world peace,
No one's against anyone
And no one shall be
Thin or obese.

Aaron Jinks (12)
Ruskin Sports College

I Have A Dream

The government shouldn't spend
So much money on weapons for wars,
When they could donate so much of it
To Third World countries.

People shouldn't be afraid
To walk out of their own homes
Like some people are because
They're scared of something happening to them.

People shouldn't be racist to others,
They may have different coloured skin,
But that doesn't matter,
They're still human!

Everyone has dreams,
Even if they don't have a lot of money.
They hope they will come true,
Some are lucky, some aren't.
People should keep dreaming,
It may come true one day!

Niomi Suter (13)
Ruskin Sports College

Racism

Victims of racism and all forms of discrimination,
When you're black and a woman at the same time,
To a racist you have committed a crime.
Right now, racism is in its prime.
Right now, the discrimination is in its prime.
It appears wrong for them to earn a dime.
It appears wrong for them to be in the limelight.

Michael Bradshaw (13)
Ruskin Sports College

World Peace

Why are we in a world
Wrapped up in greed?
Can't anyone see
There are people in need?

People that are alive,
But don't even know.
People that live a life of starvation,
We should join together as one nation.

If there was no religion,
There'd be no need for war,
No need for expensive bombs,
So let's not spend any more.

How can we make this
World a better place?
No matter how big or small,
Or the colour of your face.

If we had no possessions,
There'd be nothing to share,
Nothing to fight over, but now . . .
I declare

I have a dream
That there are no haters,
No complainers or debaters!
Embrace the culture
And keep learning about others!

Save our world!

Jemma Daw (13)
Ruskin Sports College

World Peace

Racism is wrong,
The victim has to be strong.
If someone is gay,
You don't have to say
What you think in your mind.
It may not be kind,
Always think before you judge,
Even if you have a grudge.
Everyone is prejudiced,
Some worse than others,
We should all be united as brothers.
One day every racist
Will be gone, they won't exist.
If the world all came as one,
There would be no reason to drop a bomb.
I wish everyone could share,
Some people are full of greed,
Even though there is no need.
People should respect each other,
Everyone should have the freedom,
Civil rights, we surely need them.

Tamsin Waring (13)
Ruskin Sports College

I Had A Dream

I had a dream,
A dream about world peace,
No wars, no crime, no bullying,
And positively no disease.

It was a calm, peaceful world,
With fresh, clean air,
A lovely British countryside,
With the weather as a glare.

As the school bell rang,
All the children got along,
There was no unfair bullying,
They were happily singing a song.

All countries were at peace,
No crimes, no bullies, no wars,
Everyone was happy,
Everyone obeyed the laws.

I had a dream,
A dream about world peace,
No wars, no crime, no bullying,
And positively no disease.

Emily Whyatt (12)
Sandbach High School

Our Natural Disasters

The world keeps changing, every day,
Not always in the nicest way.
Tsunamis, tornados or an earthquake,
Our natural disasters, but so hard to take.

How can we stop these, what can we do?
The answers are there, with me and with you.
Recycle your paper; use your water wise,
Our natural disasters that we all despise.

We've all heard of stories about global warming,
Will the birds stop flying and the bees stop swarming?
Beautiful things disappear from our eyes,
Our natural disasters, *we need to get wise!*

It's so sad to say, but time's getting short,
We should all pay attention and give lots of thought.
The things that we waste, please keep this in mind,
Must all be reduced for the sake of mankind.

So let's work together, let's work as a team,
At the close of the day we will all find our dream.
Our planet is sacred; a new day is dawning,
Before it's too late, listen to God's warning.

Rebecca Dimond (12)
Sandbach High School

I Have A Dream . . .

The world can take a small amount of happiness
But everlasting hate.
Why? I ask, but the answer will never come, it never will.
Life is planned like a game and happiness is not one of its pieces,
Yet hope is, it is strong and growing,
So never doubt, but hope, and the answer will come.

Rebecca Barker (12)
Sandbach High School

Think Of A World

The world is a wondrous place
The birds they sing, innocent, carefree
The sun shines down with smiles all around
Tears and pain do not exist

Friendship, understanding, smiles bold
Love and kindness all around
In people's eyes, the world is a treasure
Like china, so precious, bright

But look past the window that shields your eyes
There the trouble lies
Horror is the world
Poverty, depression, starvation, death

Countries at war months on end
Starving orphans walk the streets
Acts of racism happening each day
Suffering that never ends

But think of a world so content
Where you can walk through your door
Without fear of guns, knives, bombs, death
No lying, stealing, deceit

A world without poverty
Disease, death served on a plate
Hunger, a beast feeding on life
Insufferable pain, no care

A world without feeling or compassion
The world in ruins, only us to blame
Our guilt hangs, like a shadow forever
Only we can change what has been done

Make a difference today, change your ways
Think of a world, make it, for you have to live in it.

Katie Bristow (12)
Sandbach High School

I Have A Dream

Reflected in the crystal,
I see a great world
Where people live in harmony,
Black and white, men and women.

There is no poverty,
There is help for the sick,
The weak are not mocked,
In the world of the crystal ball.

That world is not real.
These problems still exist.
The crystal is in fragments,
That world is nothing but a dream.

But dreams can come true,
The lonely can have friends,
The sad can be consoled,
The crystal can be repaired.

Cast aside your differences,
Just look at what's the same,
We are all equal,
It's not too late.

Everyone can do their part,
The planet can be saved
And with it, the people
Of the world.

Emily Birch (11)
Sandbach High School

I Have A Dream

I have a dream,
That one day people will be free,
From racism and war,
Just listen and you'll see.

The terrible things,
That happen on this Earth,
We all take advantage,
But realise what it's worth.

Racism and bullying,
Is wrong and cruel,
It doesn't make you tough,
It makes you a fool.

War and murder,
Terrorists and bombing,
Are not natural causes,
So stop them all coming.

I have a dream that one day,
People will not be judged by their skin colour,
But judged by their personalities instead,
So we all like each other and respect each other.

So that is my dream that I want the most,
To live in a world of peace and hope.
That black and white are reunited again,
So please won't you try and help me, my friend?

Hanna Blakeman (12)
Sandbach High School

My Dream

I dream of a world,
With no crime and no fear,
I dream of a world,
With no fags and no beer!
I dream of a world,
Where resources are shared,
I dream of a world
Where no children are scared.

When my world is for real,
There will be no more wars,
When my world is for real,
We'll be safe out of doors.
My world is as brave,
As a loyal dog's heart,
My world is as bright,
As a new work of art.

I wish I could go,
To my world of no fear,
Pollution a myth,
With no fags and no beer.
No worries or mess
In this wonderful place,
My only small planet,
Here in outer space.

So I look at my world,
And now I can't see,
Why can't my world be real
For you and for me?

Victoria Lockett (12)
Sandbach High School

I Have A Dream

I'm sitting silently on the floor,
Staring sadly at the door
Playing with my straw-like hair,
Knowing that my dad will soon be there
Holding his belt in his sweaty palm,
Ready to do some dreadful harm.

The door crashes open around half-nine,
I'm looking at the clock, counting time
My dad comes in, then stands still,
I'm slowly gasping, rehearsing my will
I think this time I might actually die,
Tears are trickling from my eye.

Why he hurts me I do not know,
Because every night he plans to go
Down to buy drugs from the bar,
Piling them up inside his car
So eventually, when he does get home,
All he does is hurt me and moan.

This is a terrifying nightmare,
But hardly anyone does care
It's like looking through some crystal glass,
Where nothing bad will ever pass
It takes so much to change this,
But to change it, that's my wish.

To change a nightmare to a dream,
It takes a lot to be seen
But without any help,
Without yourself,
It will never stop and become a
Dream.

Jessica Quayle (12)
Sandbach High School

I Just Can't Stop Dreaming . . .

I just can't stop dreaming that one day there will be world peace,
That we will respect each other how we know we should,
And maybe that one day there will be no murder,
No need for jail or police,

I just can't stop dreaming that one day there will be no such words
As violence,
No terrorists, no kidnaps or hit and run,
I really hope that some day people won't fear
That unsuspected silence,

I just can't stop dreaming that one day people will walk our streets
Without fear,
Without the thought of being abused or mugged,
I wish it could be a socialising place,
Not a place to be scared of what's near,

I just can't stop dreaming that one day there will be no wars,
No weapons of mass destruction,
No suicide bombers or dynamite,
At night people shouldn't have to fear the great outdoors.

Natalie Conde (12)
Sandbach High School

I Have A Dream . . .

I have a dream . . .
To climb the highest mountain,
To sail all seven seas
And to help the poor and needy,
I'm always there to please,
If only I could have this dream,
To make the world a better place,
No more war and hatred,
I would replace it
With love
And peace.

Jamie-Lee Barker (11)
Sandbach High School

I Have A Dream

Hit,
Punch.
Knuckle,
Crunch.
A bully strikes
After school.
In the yard,
Their fist as a tool.

One sprained wrist,
Two black eyes.
A broken nose,
Told to lie.

'Help!' she cries,
Yet no one hears.
I have a dream
To get rid of those fears.

Zoë Hardman (12)
Sandbach High School

I Had A Dream

I had a dream
I was miserable and sad
I had a grey cloud over my head
The sun had died and the moon came alive
I was hurt, hurt deep down
Nobody could help with my sour sound
Except one night I was alone
And an angel came down
No ordinary angel with a halo round her head
She came to me and lifted up my head
She put a smile upon my face
She said, 'Away with that miserable face
I love you and you love me because
I am your guardian angel.'

Amy Thorley (11)
Sandbach High School

Where Will You Be?

Where will you be,
When I'm all alone,
Drowning my sorrows,
Sad in my tone?

Where will you be,
When I collapse,
Lost in my world,
On a relapse?

Where will you be,
When I hit the lows,
Can go no further,
Fed up of these shows?

Where will you be,
When I can't see,
Lost in the shadow,
Or stood with me?

Where will you be,
In ten years' time,
Out of my mind,
Or still in this rhyme?

Where will I be
In ten years' time?
Maybe, just like you,
Inspiring this rhyme.

Nadine Thornton (14)
Sandbach High School

I Have A Dream

As I lay fast asleep at night,
Staring up above my head,
A dream came creeping to my head,
It dragged me across oceans and out of my bed,

Mysterious stars shone into my eyes,
Planets and galaxies circled the skies,
Down below on Earth creatures let out their cries,

And I was carried further out into space,
Oblivious to the cries of the human race,
A force pulling me there to find a better place,

Until, on a glistening planet, I stopped to stare,
At the glorious inhabitants living there,
And the thrilling sensations gathered in the air,

My feet touched the ground and a dragon came near,
A creature so beautiful, yet I cowered with fear,
But the kindness on its face was so charmingly dear,

It called to a unicorn, a faerie and an elf,
They approached us so quietly with incredible stealth,
And they stood there proudly.

They spoke as one, 'In many years this realm will be gone,
But your homeland will be filled with scorn,
So we give you the gift to save it from hate,
To keep it peaceful 'till a later date'.'

Each shed a tear which in my hand gleamed,
They said goodbye and my dazzled eyes witnessed
A change of scene,
The universe told me: 'Remember your dream.'

And I woke in my bed,
Staring up above my head,
Clutching the purest crystal,
From my dream.

Rebecca Drake (11)
Sandbach High School

If Only . . .

If only people could be treated fairly,
All world leaders could call a truce,
If only no one in the world would suffer,
And prisoners of war could all be set loose.

If only money was non-existent,
If only the world was peaceful and fair,
If the prevention of starvation was a top priority,
If only everyone would really care.

If only everyone would truly realise,
That humans should be treated equally,
If only they would stop polluting the world,
And leave it the way it was meant to be.

If only everything was perfect,
If only we could respect our amazing Earth,
The world, a place of wonders,
If only we could treat it for what it is worth . . .

Eleanor Swinnerton (11)
Sandbach High School

My Dream

I have a dream to be a footballer
But I'd hate to be a gambler
They drink and smoke
Then go broke

I have a dream to be a footballer
Lifting the Cup for England
I have a dream to be a footballer
And score the winning goal against Finland

I have a dream to be a footballer
Running out on the pitch as the captain
I have a dream to be a footballer.

Chloé Beadle (12)
Sandbach High School

I Have A Dream

I have a dream,
That white and black will come together,
Stop racism, poverty and hate forever,
And realise the colour of your skin doesn't matter,
What's inside will stop the clatter.

I have a dream,
That old and young will be befriended,
And feelings of niceness will be recommended,
And all living creatures will be treated as one,
But half the battle is yet to be won.

I have a dream,
That happiness will fall in the rain,
And we will be rid of hunger and pain,
Though, sadly enough, the rain will go away,
But no matter what happens the puddles will stay.

Madison Dunn (11)
Sandbach High School

My Dream

Guns banging everywhere.
People scared all around,
Scared for the family,
Scared for themselves,
Hiding in the smallest crevice.

Silence at last.
No more noise,
Trucks and bombs stop.
Listen, silence and stillness,
War has ceased.

Busy people rebuilding lives,
No more destruction for the city.
Creating something better than before.
Different people working together,
Making peace for the world.

Georgina Bell (12)
Sandbach High School

I Have A Dream

M y dream is for happiness
Y elling and screaming is a thing of the past

D isagreeing will be for good reasons
R adiance will be encouraged
E ars will be used for the good
A nother day has just gone by
M oaning will be replaced by praising

I have a dream
S preading happiness over the world

H iding away will be gone for good
A nimals will have rights as well
P oachers can't destroy their lives
P eople's sins will be forgiven
I llnesses will be cured, no matter what
N o one can destroy people's pride
E ven if they try and try
S tirring up trouble will not be accepted
S o people can live a life that's full.

Simran Davegun (12)
Sandbach High School

I Have A Dream

Over the world I flew,
Over wealth, peace and health,
Where everybody was friends,
That was my dream.

Over happy, playful children everywhere,
Where unity and equality rule,
Where racism, hunger, hate, injustice and famine are dead,
That was my dream,

Over the forest,
Crooked branches tore at me,
Down I fell,
Down and down,

Down through the roof of a car,
Up I jerked,
Down to reality,
Gazed at the scenery flying past,
Oh, if only!

Laura Baty (11)
Sandbach High School

I Have A Dream

I'm flying high above the world,
Without a thought for what's below,
Until I look down to the planet
And see the horrors which lie there.
Neglect,
Loneliness,
Poverty,
Innocent people dying,
And what for?
Because they look different from the next person,
Or because they have a different faith?
It makes me sad to think that some people
Look down on others different to them.
But I have a dream,
A dream that one day there will be world peace,
No one will criticise anyone else.
People will want to share and be kind,
No one will feel hate,
But sometimes I ask myself,
'Will this ever happen?'

Elizabeth Firth (12)
Sandbach High School

Last Night I Had A Dream

Last night I had a dream,
A dream I'll never forget,
I dreamt about my future thoughts;
Thoughts I won't forget;

They were bad thoughts
And sad thoughts,
Thoughts I wanted to do
If you're quiet and listen carefully,
I'll share my dream with you;

I dreamt of climbing mountains,
I dreamt of sailing seas,
I dreamt of strolling deserts,
And walking through the trees;

I have spread my dreams under your feet,
Tread softly because you tread on my dreams!

Olivia Cole (11)
Sandbach High School

My Dream

I had a dream, a wonderful dream,
That everyone in the world acted as a team
And made poverty history . . .
But that seems like a total mystery
If you're sitting there
Thinking, glancing and having a stare.
Think of others
Who have no brothers
Food, they think
Every time they blink,
'Peace one day'
Some do say

What will happen next?

Charlotte Harrison (11)
Sandbach High School

I Have A Dream

Close your eyes,
squeeze them tight.
What am I going
to dream tonight?

Am I living in fantasy,
or could it just be real?
Is it just a nightmare,
I don't know what to feel.

Will I be angry?
Will I be sad?
Will I be happy
or will I be mad?

Have a dream to change your life,
have a dream to die.
Have a dream to fly the world,
or have a dream to lie.

Rebecca Westwater (11)
Sandbach High School

I Have A Dream

I have a dream that we will have peace,
That weapons and war will cease,
We need a land that we can cleanse,
And all of the rivals should be friends.

I have a dream . . .

I have a dream that the fighting will stop,
Instead, we should see the rabbits hop,
With no more illness or poverty,
In the field of peace and tranquillity.

I have a dream . . .

Andy Small (12)
The King's School, Chester

I Have A Dream

I have a dream
That one day freedom will ring.
I have a dream
That one day we will sing.
Let freedom ring.

I can see a day
When we can walk together, hand in hand.
I can see a day
When we will walk together, hand in hand.
Let freedom ring.

You will know that day
There will be a day
When freedom will ring.

Tom Menzies (13)
The King's School, Chester

I Have A Dream

I have a dream,
A thought in my head.
I think about it when I go to bed.
I lie down and close my eyes,
And enter a world full of magic and surprise.

A world not known to this one here,
A world which seems not able to appear.
A world of happiness, fun and joy,
A world that's not treated as a toy.
A world that loves, with people that care,
A world that knows and does not dare.
A world that is only known to me,
A world that is kind, wild and free.

This world ends when I open my eyes,
My mum wakes me up and my dream dies.
The world which we have today, I see again
Until the sky darkens and my mind plays its game.

Elizabeth Ellen Roberts (13)
The King's School, Chester

I Have A Dream

I have a dream,
That one day, there will be no war.
No blown-up house without a floor.
That poverty will pass and go.
I hope we've reached the final blow.

I have a dream,
That the world will be a better place.
To save the world and its race,
And what was good shall return,
As all the world's evil begins to burn.

I have a dream,
That the green grass shall cover the ground,
As the sun's rays kiss the ground.
That lakes will fill with water for all,
And trees around grow green and tall.

I have a dream,
Where we live in a place of peace,
As guns and bombs begin to cease.
Where children can run, jump and play.
Why don't we change: what do you say?

Richard Charles Wynne (13)
The King's School, Chester

I Have A Dream

I have a dream that everyone can believe in himself or herself.
I have a dream that we will all be accepted equal.
Just because of our colour, it doesn't mean that we aren't all
God's children.
I have a dream that there will be no more drugs on this Earth
and that no one will see anymore drugs in this world.
I have a dream that no one will make fun of each other
just because they are so slow, dumb or handicapped.
I have a dream that one day everyone will love each other,
no matter what they look like.

Will Simmonds (13)
The King's School, Chester

I Have A Dream

I have a dream,
A dream, a reality-filled dream,
A dream where everyone does well in exams,
Where everyone succeeds in their plans.

I have a dream,
A dream in which anyone can do anything,
A dream where you make yourself who you are.
We call this dream, 'Life'.

I have a dream,
A dream after life,
Where other people control how and where you exist,
We call this dream, 'Death'.

I have a dream,
A dream where war doesn't rule,
A dream where 9/11 never happened,
We call this dream, 'A fantasy'.

James Oldman (14)
The King's School, Chester

I Had A Dream

I had a dream that dreams would come true.
The world was a fantasy, a legend and a myth.
Monsters and dragons outside great city walls
Cyclopses clashing with Minotaurs, good vs evil.
Adventures and exploring in this wonderful world
The dream seemed like it could never end,
As in films and books, things just seemed to be there,
Where there were no breaks from fun, just action all the time.
It was a shame it had to end, the adventure was only getting started,
My dream was too good to be true
But I know it will happen again very soon, so no need to worry.

Ed Corbett (11)
The King's School, Chester

Dream Cinema

Alarms ring,
People awake,
Cogs turn,
Electrons flow,
Workers clean,
Staff set up,
Refreshments loaded,
Crowds gather,
Lights blind,
Doors open,
People enter,
Noise builds,
Staff serve,
People chat,
Lights die,
Curtains open.

The projector is on,
The dreams begin.

Joe Hollingworth (12)
The King's School, Chester

I Have A Dream

I have a dream
Of walking by a stream,
Children playing in the grass,
Regardless of their class,
Black, brown and white,
No longer do they fight,
Harmony is here,
Between all those I hold dear,
I have a dream.

Kallum Marsden (12)
The King's School, Chester

My Dream

I have a dream
A dream that will bring us together
I have a dream
Of friendship for now and forever

And with this dream
We will stand up and fight for each other
And with this dream
We shall become, not foes but brothers

This dream must be
If we're to become a great nation
This dream must be
Built upon firmest foundation

I have a dream
A dream that will bring us together
I have a dream
Of friendship for now and forever.

Jenny Corlett (11)
The King's School, Chester

People's Dreams

People have dreams
Which let their imagination flow.
People have dreams
Which let their minds glow.

People have dreams
Where they're ever so glad.
People have dreams
Where they may be very sad.

We all have dreams
That we may always remember.
We all have dreams
From January to December.

Emily Guest (12)
The King's School, Chester

I Have A Dream

I have a dream . . .
Badgers scuttling around in the woods,
Hippos rolling over in the mud,
Moles digging, digging for their lives,
Life in the countryside really starts to thrive.

Walking through the densely packed forest,
Watching the squirrels burying their nuts,
Leaves rustling, rustling underfoot,
As I watch the world go by.

Then all of a sudden, out of the blue,
I turn into a red Swiss roll.
And I do roll, down a steep cliff face,
Into a pot of purple custard.

Yet it isn't a pot of purple custard,
It's a space tardis,
And I end up in space, all alone in space,
Yet I'm not alone . . .

And I'm not red anymore either!
I turn yellow with pink spots,
And as I look up I see, I really do see,
A giant marshmallow frog.

So I run, only I don't . . . I roll,
Swiss rolls can't run, you know!
But I don't roll quick enough, oh no I don't,
And I meet my sticky end with the marshmallow frog!

Siobhan Barnard (13)
The King's School, Chester

I Have A Dream

I have a dream,
I could be a queen
Or am I a king?
Or can I sing?
I have a dream.

I have a dream,
I could be in a daydream,
Dreaming about pretty things,
And strange human beings,
I have a dream.

I have a dream,
I could be paddling upstream,
Battling out with feisty waves,
Until I find a cosy cave,
I have a dream.

I have a dream,
I could be shouting and screaming,
At a loud music concert,
In my favourite T-shirt,
I have a dream.

I have a dream,
I could be looking at the stars' glowing gleam,
Flying through all space,
I had better retrace,
I have a dream.

Kathryn Williams (13)
The King's School, Chester

I Have A Dream

I've had dreams,
Dreams of glory,
Dreams of sadness,
I've had dreams of ambition.

I once dreamt of being an astronaut,
To explore the stars,
I dreamt that I could be the first person
To draw the Earth on the moon,
I dreamt I could discover new planets,
New civilisations, but then,

I dreamt of being a doctor,
A saver of many lives,
The conqueror of illness,
Helpful to people of all kinds,
To help the sick, that was my dream, until

I started playing tennis,
A sport full of fun,
To beat a ball to death and not save it for one,
To be the best in the world,
The greatest of all time, and then,

I realised that my real dream is to be happy in life,
However that may be.

Serge Alain Osula (13)
The King's School, Chester

Dreams

Every good woman and every great man
Has had a dream; a master plan.
Dreams start journeys,
Challenges and missions.
You won't get anywhere without a vision.

In the Bible,
Pharaoh had a dream.
He asked Joseph, 'What does it mean?'
He answered Pharaoh and got it right.
From then on he had a better life.

Martin Luther King from the USA
Dreamed of a world without racial hate
Where you wouldn't be restricted
By the colour of your skin,
Where to talk to a black man was not the greatest sin.

Everyone has dreams,
Everyone can be great.
But take your opportunities
Don't leave it too late.
Jump every hurdle and pass every test.
Then you'll be great; you'll be the best
At sport, music or being on TV,
Or maybe even for poetry!

Jack Webb (13)
The King's School, Chester

I Have A Dream

I had a dream that I had a clone,
A funny second me.
I had a dream that I had a phone
From the future yet to be.

I had a dream of the Grim Reaper,
As scary as can be.
He changed from Grim Reaper to a creeper
Hey! Isn't that worse for me?

Anyway, I had a dream about a palace
Great, it's all for me.
Diving into my swimming pool
As happy as can be.

Splash!

Alex Howe (13)
The King's School, Chester

Dreams

I had a dream. We all have dreams.
A sleep of dreams. Warm, cosy, happy,
Not real. Not unreal.
Then waking. Reality. Dawn.

He had a dream. A dream he shared with us,
A dream of equality. Cold, harsh, misery.
He worked. He spoke.
Then fighting. Marching. Peace.

Matt Robinson (14)
The King's School, Chester

I Had A Dream Last Night

I had a dream last night
That adults were kids in disguise
Vegetables were bad for you
And washing up damaged your health

I had a dream last night
That it snowed every day
Sweets were part of a staple diet
And mums didn't really know best

I had a dream last night
That aunts didn't give you socks for xmas
Grandad didn't snore in his chair
And the moon was really made of cheese

I had a dream last night
That the TV remote never left my hand
Big brothers didn't exist
And chips were always on the menu

I had a dream last night
That McDonald's was a regular outing
It never rained at weekends
And my team always won!

I wish you didn't have to grow up!

Kate Phillipson (14)
The King's School, Chester

I Had A Dream

I had a dream
I was flying,
I had a dream
I was free,
I had a dream
Everyone was equal,
I had a dream
There were no rich and poor,
I had a dream,
There was no such thing as war,
I had a dream
No one died,
I had a dream
I could live forever,
I had a dream,
I could cure all illness,
I had a dream,
I could help more people,
I had a dream
Where people were never harmed,
I had a dream
Humans and animals could communicate,
I had a dream
I could climb the highest mountain,
I had a dream
I could walk on clouds . . .
I had a dream . . .
A very interesting dream!

Lucy Butterfield (11)
The King's School, Chester

My Dream

I had a dream,
About what, it would seem,
Leaves me a feeling of dread.
And then I think and say to myself,
It's really all in your head.

Then when I ask,
What does this dream mean?
The memory wipes clean,
And I can't remember what I said!

It kind of annoys me,
The thought flies in and out of my head.
What can it be
That I hate to see?

Will I ever know?
Does it ever show?
I cannot know.
I fear the dream will never let go!

When I go to bed at night,
The dream again takes flight.
I have death within my sight.
And then I laugh and say,
'Go away'
It obeys and leaves me in shock.

And from that day on,
The dream was gone.
And I thought
That it was just stupid!

Tom Marquis (13)
The King's School, Chester

I Have A Dream

Every night,
I have a dream,
Beginning to end,
A recurring scene.

I have this dream,
Like a boring play,
In winter or spring,
September or May.

I think it's of,
What I will become,
But if it's my future,
It's not much fun.

I always remember what I have dreamt,
Especially the colours and shapes,
Red and green zigzags,
Like the computer's mistakes.

It sounds very silly,
It sounds deranged,
This muddled-up dream,
It sounds very strange.

At least my dream,
Is more exciting than school,
There are no questions,
And I'm no fool.

I dream that some day,
I'll know what it means,
That squiggly, strange
Weird, deranged dream!

Miranda Harle (11)
The King's School, Chester

I Have A Dream

I have a dream that the world shall be freed of all evil,
In order to make the world a better place.
From medieval times and beyond,
Further than deep space.
A dream is hope,
All dreams are all hope.

I have a dream that sunlight shall shine throughout the world,
In order to make the world a better place.
All sunlight unfurled,
To abolish all darkness with grace.
Get rid of dark,
Light up with a spark.

I have a dream that the world shall be free of all problems,
In order to make the world a better place.
Goodbye all problems!
As King laid it down, we should embrace
The problems now,
And men will say, 'Wow!'

I have a dream that goodness shall fill the unclear future,
In order to make the world a better place.
Dreams are the future.
Goodwill shall grow and leave not a trace
Of things not right
That could make us fight

I have a dream that many more people shall have more dreams,
In order to make the world a better place.
The world shall have dreams,
Dreams that have hope and put forward a case.
I have a dream,
You shall have a dream.

Matt Ireland (13)
The King's School, Chester

I Have A Dream

I have a dream,
A dream of a nation,
Free from racist
Scrutinisation.

Free from comments,
On the colour of skin,
Where black is just the blindfold,
Hiding who is within.

I have a dream,
Where all men could,
Sit together at the table
Of brotherhood.

And in this dream,
God's children unite,
Together! Regardless
Of black or white.

I have a vision,
Where everyone is free,
From the clutches of racism,
Imprisoning this dream,

I have a dream today!

Daniel Axelsson (14)
The King's School, Chester

I Have A Dream

I have a dream that one day
My world will be peaceful,
Countries will not go to war, trouble will be erased.

I have a dream that one day
People will respect each other
And colour will not mean prejudice and discrimination.

I have a dream that soon
My world will unite
And religion will not tear us apart.

I have a personal dream - to live
Life as a challenge and an adventure,
A dream to live fully and not just exist.

One day, I will rise
Above my expectations
And look back with pride.

I shall savour success.

I have a dream that
Once I reach my goals, I will be able
To help others and ease their pain.

But most of all . . .
I have a dream to be myself,
To always be an individual.

Edward Andrade (13)
The King's School, Chester

Just A Dream

I had a dream a while ago,
Where I sat on a grassy hill,
There I watched the shimmering stream flow,
I woke up, perched on my window sill,
I looked out at the industrial scene,
And I realised my dream, was just a dream.

I had a dream a while ago,
Where no one would steal or kill,
Where laws were set, everyone would follow,
I woke up, perched on my window sill,
I looked out at the murder scene,
And I realised my dream, was just a dream.

I had a dream a while ago,
Where you could learn at your will,
Where to find friends, you didn't have far to go,
I woke up, perched on my window sill,
I looked out at the school scene,
And I realised my dream, was closer than it seemed.

Hattie Webb (11)
The King's School, Chester

I Had A Dream

I had a dream when I was small,
I'll remember it when I'm grown and tall.
When I'm grown and tall,
I'll remember the dream I had when I was small.

Katherine Pierce (11)
The King's School, Chester

I Have A Dream

I have a dream I do, to have a successful life,
I have a dream to be the perfect mother and wife,
And when I'm bored I watch the clock tick past,
Not realising that it could be my last.

I have a dream I do, I have a dream, dream, dream.

I have a dream I do, I am an astronaut,
Flying high in the sky, counting the stars I've caught,
I have a dream I do, I am a ballet dancer,
I can be soaring through the air,
With the wind in my hair.

I have a dream I do, I have a dream, dream, dream.

I have a dream I do, that I can wake up from my dream,
But there I am in the middle of a stream,
I close my eyes so tight they're bleeding,
And all of a sudden I'm in a war, leading!

I have a dream I do, I have a dream, dream, dream.

I have a dream I do, I live to 107,
It seems so far away from just 11!

Megan Rudge (11)
The King's School, Chester

I Have A Dream

I have a dream,
Of life being perfect,
But it can never happen.

Josh Roberts (11)
The King's School, Chester

I Have A Dream

Oppression,
Depression,
Rejection,
No affection,
Degradation,
Segregation,
I have a dream,
To be heard and seen.

No judgement on races,
Of colours of faces,
Forget my religion,
When you make your decision on me,
Judge on personality.

To sit where I choose on a bus,
To go to school where it's not them and us,
To eat where I like,
Whether black or white,
To be happy and proud,
And to cry out loud,
I have achieved my dream,
I am heard and seen.

Rory Benson (12)
The King's School, Chester

I Have A Dream

I have a dream,
That repeats and repeats.
And this is always seen,
When I am fast asleep.

I have a dream,
An owl is hooting by,
Over clouds I lean,
As I drift over the moonlit sky.

I have a dream,
I am among the many beautiful stars.
Over the moon I have been,
I think I can see Mars.

I have a dream
The houses are tiny from up here
The sun is being mean,
Because daylight is near.

I had a dream,
It's now time to get out of bed.
I am now hopeful and so keen,
That these will be forever in my head.

Ashleigh Milner (11)
The King's School, Chester

Dream

Winter is here - the wind and rain,
So glad I'm safe in bed.
The wind is rattling the windowpane,
My pillow cradling my head.

Soon I drop off into deep sleep,
Strange thoughts begin to form -
Images of storms and floods so deep,
A ship caught in a storm.

I find myself on the deck of a ship,
Fear in my stomach, a quiver on my lip.
To the starboard side the deck begins to tip,
Into the water I see the sails slip.

I feel myself falling - no one around,
Storm still blowing in the background.
But on my bedroom carpet I am found.
My window is wide open - the ship's run aground.

Sam Wilson (13)
The King's School, Chester

I Have A Dream

I have a dream to climb the stars.
I have a dream to explore the unexplored
and fly like a dove over the sea,
my beak skimming the waves,
the wind in my face.
I have a dream of freedom,
to live where and when I want,
to see the past and future.
I want to explore life at its full glory.
I want to solved unsolved questions
and give unknown answers.
But I can't do any of that.
Deep down, I dream to be myself.

Charles Geary (12)
The King's School, Chester

I Have A Dream

I have a dream that the world will start anew,
That all the buildings are gone,
And streams, rivers and meadows are as they once were,
I have a dream that all people will be free and treated equally,
That there are no rules or laws, only your free will,
And you can do as you please.
I have a dream that everyone will be happy and cherish every
minute of life,
Where birds and beasts are at peace with humans,
And the Earth is clean and flowers and plants blossom everywhere.
I have a dream that there is no fighting or war,
There is no poverty, slavery or imprisonment,
And where we live off the land and eat what we grow and
there is no money or government.
I have a dream that children play and run across fields and
in streams,
Without their parents needing to worry about them,
And that there is no crime, punishment or torturing.
I have a dream that the world is safe,
That everywhere you look, makes you want to smile
And there is colour everywhere.
I have a dream that I can conquer mountains,
That I can solve everyone's problems,
And keep the entire world at peace.
I have a dream that the oceans are clean and the water is fresh,
Where we don't need to move because we are happy where we are,
And that we never want more and we are content with what we have,
I have a dream that we love the world and care for it like a child,
Where we do not throw litter and pollute the air,
And that we keep the world as if it is still new,

I have a dream . . . but it is only a dream!

Vicky Wilson-Theaker (12)
The King's School, Chester

He Had A Dream

He had a dream of complete equality between men.
No more the poverty that ruled Negro existence.
To banish the manacles of segregation and exile,
And unify the nation, despite its resistance.
The promise of the 'Declaration of Independence',
Held back from the citizens of colour,
Leaving them to suffer from racial injustice,
When the white man should call them his brother.

He had a dream of freedom for his people,
Gained in dignity, without hatred and bitterness.
To trust white men despite past oppression,
And walk with them in togetherness.
Started so long before as another man's ideal.
Nothing had changed in the black man's position.
The poverty, the isolation, the discrimination,
Pushed to the edge of society, treated with derision.

He had a dream that God's children could live as one.
Attitudes have changed as the years have passed.
Has America's promise of liberty been fulfilled?
Have his dreams come true? Are they free at last?

William Moreland (13)
The King's School, Chester

I Have A Dream

I have a dream about love and peace
A dream that will never, never cease
I have a dream about truth and delight
A dream that captivates me every night

I have a dream about achieving my goals
A dream that cleans and cleanses the soul
I have a dream that I can learn
A dream for which I yearn and yearn

I have a dream about people who are kind
A dream that stays transfixed in my mind
I have a dream of loving and giving
A dream in which others are forgiving

I have a dream of receiving love
A dream that will come from above
I have a dream to be up 'there'
A dream that is happy, without care

I have a dream about becoming free
A dream I long to become reality
I have a dream to make a new start
A dream that will always be in my heart.

Katrina Holbrook (12)
The King's School, Chester

I Had A Dream

I had a dream that I lived in a tasty land of chocolate.
When I felt hungry my arm looked a treat, so now
I have half an arm.
My pet cat was brown and white or should I say milk and white.
This land blew me away.
There was Fudge Town, White City, Milk Street
And for the adults, Belgian Choc Village.
People never went hungry and never got fat.
Except for Bill.
More people started to become ill.
Their stomachs couldn't cope.
People were dying.
Except for Bill.
I am dead now and everyone is a ghost.
No one lives in that dream anymore.
Except for Bill.

Jack Taylor (12)
The King's School, Chester

I Have A Dream

I have a dream,
And it all feels real.
My mind is sent to another place,
Where anything can happen,
I could become a millionaire
And buy anything I want.
I could be a king
And have people bow to me.
I could be famous
And have a driven limo.

But then something wakes me up,
And I'm back in my bed.
It was all just a dream
And all in my head.

Ross Alexander (14)
The King's School, Chester

I Have A Dream

I saw a stone,
So cold and hard.
When I touched the stone,
I saw a bright star shard.
The world is cold,
When your soul has been sold.
As a slave you obey,
And do as you are told.
There could be a hope,
But you have to be bold.
By working hard,
You could buy back your soul.
Only a fool,
Would be so cruel,
To keep a man as a toy,
Everyone has a right to joy.
I saw a stone,
So cold and hard.
When I touched the stone,
I saw a bright star shard.

Tom Stables (11)
The King's School, Chester

I Have A Dream

I have a dream I will have a life of simplicity
I have a dream I will have a life of laughter
I have a dream I will be treated with equality
I have a dream I will be loved for being me
I have a dream I will find true friendship
I have a dream I will have a life of love
I have a dream I will not stray off the path of life
I have a dream I will have a life that is pure
I have a dream I will live up to my heart's desires.

Millie Johnson (11)
The King's School, Chester

I Have A Dream

I have a dream,
That there is
A really cool school,
Where children laugh and play.

Our teachers will be,
Jack Black as the head,
Gene Simmons as the music teacher,
And the desks made of lead.

Albert Einstein for maths,
JK Rowling for English,
Isaac Newton for science,
And every teacher has to wash a dish.

Jac Chirac for French,
Bill Gates for IT,
The Pope for RS,
Some teachers learn Tai Chi.

Christopher Columbus for geography,
Ronaldinho for games,
Julius Caesar for Latin,
None of these will use canes.

Picasso for art,
Delia Smith for the lunches,
This is the ideal school,
Where days don't end in violent punches.

Owen Dawson (12)
The King's School, Chester

If I Had A Dream

If I had a dream
In which I was rich
I'd want to one day
Own a football pitch

In my dream I'd buy
The best team around
To train and play in
My new football ground

As the goalkeeper
I'd dream of playing
Making great saves by
Jumping and diving

Every match played
Would to us be vital
I'd dream we could win
Every Cup and title

In the Premier League
We would be the best
Champions, I'd dream
Better than the rest

But until the day
When my dream comes true
With just supporting
Man United I'll make do!

Matthew Burgess (11)
The King's School, Chester

I Have A Dream

(Hell in the trenches: World War I)

I am here in the trenches,
It is very cold.

The rain thunders on the ground,
Just like the bullets.

I am hungry and thirsty,
The food is running out.

The mud grows ever thicker,
I am drenched and dirty.

I fight for my country,
My Prime Minister and people.

I dream of my home,
Warm and inviting.

But I know I will never get back there,
It tears me apart inside.

The German shells and bullets,
Raining down on me.

Soldiers' limbs flying past,
The shells are exploding.

I am fighting in the field,
Destined to die.

A cold, hard rain of bullets,
I fall to the ground.

In my mind I see someone,
It's my family crying.

I have a dream, a dream of home,
As I lie here dying.

Ketan Dhital (12)
The King's School, Chester

Louder Than Words

'Actions speak louder than words,'
Said one intelligent fool
And I suppose that sometimes they can
But they can cause more harm than good.
When Martin LK stood on that stage
Announcing to the world that he had a dream
Do you think the people around him were wondering
Why he wasn't making a scene?
Do you think they were thinking,
Where is the fire? Where is the noise?
While he spoke to the world
About his dream for his girls and his boys.
The answer is 'No!'
They were stood totally entranced
They didn't want him to make a show
And juggle, and sing, and dance.
They wanted to hear his vision
That the world could be better for him and for you
Because deep down in their hearts
That's all they wanted too.
That giant crowd
Listening to one man speak
Wanting to hear the vision
That one man did seek.
And when those people left at the end of the day
When they packed up their stuff and drove away
Their thoughts had been changed, not by force but by choice
And their views now different, not through action . . .
But through voice!

Pip Osmond-Williams (13)
Tytherington High School

The Future Today

While poverty wreaks the nation
The wealthy sit and stare
And carry on their happy lives
Pretend they're unaware

As death and grief control the world
The world ignores the pain
Why should we help? No one does
For what is there to gain?

As war breaks out in countries far
We disregard their cries
What difference does it make to us?
It simply passes by

We just overlook it
The death, the strife, the grief
We fail to spot the ancient rug
That it's been swept beneath

But if the tide of apathy
Will part and show the way
Then we can build a better world
And we can start today.

Eleanor Sutton (13)
Tytherington High School

The Dream

He tunes, it tunes in -
Homing through the A-Z
Of light entertainment dreams.
Seventeen years of resolution colour
Crackles through black and white:
Pitch-perfect code

Ninety-eight, ninety-nine . . .

Pressing, pushing, seeing, searching
Fingers scanning for a new mystique
Not the need to know the story
Just to dream of how it came to be.

Caitlin Doherty (15)
Tytherington High School

I Have A Dream!

I have a dream of . . .
Black and white people coming together
No prejudice!
No racism!

I have a dream of . . .
World peace!
Peace becoming a reality
No more wars!

I have a dream of . . .
People who stand up for themselves
Do not get punished!
Please help!

I have a dream of . . .
Different cultures coming together
People having enough food and drink!

Can you help my dream come true?

Demi-Leigh Maguire (12)
Verdin High School

I Have A Dream

I wish I were an NBA star,
Or maybe a rock star.
But me ma sez that I should be an MTV star,
In me bling-bling car.

I'll be the best,
Better than the rest.
I'll work with a team,
That's like a laser beam.

If I were an NBA star,
I could be like Michael Jordan, a shooting star,
If I were a rock star,
I could be like Jimmy Hendrix, a guitar star.

I'll live in a mansion,
With my lifestyle in expansion.
But if I live in a council house,
I'll be living like a mouse.

William Benjamin (12)
Verdin High School

I Have A Dream

I have a dream
That teachers fall,
The walls and
Doors and all.

I have a dream
That power will change
Kids with rules
Teachers in range

I have a dream of
Teachers in chains
And
Kids at the mains

I have a dream to
End the war
But instead
We get more

I have a dream
For it all to end
To stop suffering
Before it drives me round the bend!

Tyler Goodwin (13)
Verdin High School

I Have A Dream!

Justice
Freedom
Equality

I have a *dream* of . . .
Justice
Karma for those who sin
Murderers, thieves, punished
What comes around, goes around.

I have a *dream* of . . .
Freedom
Follow your hopes and ambitions
No one, nothing to stop you
Countries unite
Judgement has passed
Clothes and looks don't matter

I have a *dream* of . . .
Equality
Money is not an issue
Poverty is history
A bully-free world of peace and happiness
Racism does not exist

My dream is only a dream
It is us that can make it real
But for now only in my . . .
Dreams!

Jo Levis (13)
Verdin High School

I Have A Dream

I have a dream to ride the air,
On a world-famous roller coaster.
Have the wind in my face,
Overtake all the planes
And land safely at home.

I have a dream to ride the air,
On the wings of a golden eagle.
Gripping its feathers,
As we dodge through the trees,
Leaving my past behind.

I have a dream to ride the air,
On a flying unicorn.
Its eyes glisten,
As we ride through the clouds
Hoping to find the end of the rainbow.

I have a dream to ride the air,
In my own imagination.
Do what I want,
Ride what I want
As thoughts enter my body.

I have a dream to ride the air,
Or maybe climb the stairway to Heaven.
Close friends and relatives,
Welcoming me,
Someone says, 'Go, get your dream!'

Emma Louise Daniells (13)
Verdin High School

I Have A Dream

My dream is
To have my life made from gold,
And to see money wherever I go,
But what do I do
When the money runs out?

My dream is
To get away,
Live in a place where there's nothing but sun,
But what do I do
If I miss my family?

My dream is
To walk down the red carpet,
With all eyes on me,
But what do I do
If I get too busy to see my friends?

So all these dreams could go wrong!

I have a dream
For my family and friends
To live life, feeling
Happy and free,
And nothing could go wrong with that.

Jacqui Williams (13)
Verdin High School

I Have A Dream . . .

I have a dream,
That one day black and white people
Will be treated as equals.
I have a dream,
That racism will stop.
I have dreamt that this will come true.
I have a dream,
That one day wars will end
And the world will become a better place.
That one day there will be more money to go around poor people.
I have dreamt that poverty will end.
I have dreamt that it will come true.
I have a dream,
That one day the world will become peaceful
Without,
Poverty,
Racism,
And
Wars!

Make it a better place!

Bethany Jones (12)
Verdin High School

I Have A Dream

I have a dream,
that one day I will become an athlete.

I have a dream,
that one day I will run the marathon.

I have a dream,
that one day all the wars will end.

I have a dream,
that one day I will win the lottery.

I have a dream,
that one day all the schools will be closed.

I have a dream,
that one day everyone will be home-schooled.

I have a dream,
that one day racism will stop.

I have a dream,
that one day there will be no bullies.

I have a dream,
that one day everyone will be treated equally.

I have a dream today.

Rebecca Martin (13)
Verdin High School

I Have A Dream

I have a dream of freedom,
Say what you want, do what you want,
Go wherever you want to go,
Let your creativity flow.

I have a dream of animal welfare,
No hunting in hot countries,
Nor animals tortured into insanity,
Fur should not be vanity.

I have a dream of equality,
Goths and Preps make best friends,
Weirdness is normality,
Judged by personality.

I have a dream of no more famine,
Food and clean water for all,
But maybe . . .
Something for me?

I dream of lots of money,
Stacks and stacks of cash,
I dream of piles of clothes,
Designer but no fur.

I dream of?
I dream of . . .
I dream of a perfect world.

Stephanie Mander (12)
Verdin High School

I Have A Dream . . .

I have a dream,
That today addicts will stop buying cigarettes and alcohol
that kill our population.
That today, everyone, whether young or old, rich or poor,
will have an education.

I have a dream,
That today the violence will stop and all wars will die.
That today everyone in the world will love and feel loved by.

I have a dream,
That today everyone will have somewhere to call home
and a roof over their head.
That today no one shall eat junk food but everyone will be fed.

I have a dream,
That today justice will be done; we will get what we deserve,
punishment or reward!
That today black and white will be the best of friends and we will
worship our chosen Lord.

I have a dream,
That today children will be treated as humans, not punch bags
to punch.
That today our streets will be cleared of wrappers or leftover lunch.

I have a dream,
That today my dreams will come true,
Someone's got to act *today,*
My dream is to get help from you!

Olivia Osborne (12)
Verdin High School

I Have A Dream . . .

I have a dream . . .
Of discipline
Where disruptions are noticed
Troublemakers are sorted
And people can learn

I have a dream . . .
Of an unprejudiced world
Where you can be old, young,
Fat, thin, short, tall
And still be treated the same as everyone else

I have a dream . . .
Of equality and fairness
Where first appearance
Isn't what you're judged on
Where you're individual, but not different

I have a dream . . .
Of justice
Where people pay for what they have done
Where actions have consequences
Criminals no longer free to walk the streets

I have a dream . . .
A 'Goth' can be friends with a 'Chav'
A black person and a white person get along
Where criminals are where they belong
But I only have my dreams.

Megan Harrison (13)
Verdin High School

I Have A Dream

I have a dream,
There should be world peace,
Without innocent people getting slaughtered,
For doing nothing at all.

I have a dream,
There should be no more racists,
Everyone should be treated equally,
We're all the same.

I have a dream,
There should be no more litter,
It destroys the environment,
And kills many animals.

I have a dream,
For everyone to have an education,
Black or white,
Rich or poor.

I have a dream,
To stop cruelty to children,
To treat them as human beings,
Just like you and me.

I have a dream,
There should be medicines for everyone,
So they get the chance,
To live life to the full.

I have a dream,
For you to make my dreams come true.

Elaine Dudley (12)
Verdin High School

My Dream Poem

I have a dream
To be an actress
To be in a movie
To be in the press

I have a dream
That there will be no wars
But I believe that it's not us
Who are the cause

I have a dream
That I will be rich
Rather than being poor
And living in a ditch

I have a dream
There will be no global warming
So that in a hundred years
No one will be mourning

I have a dream
Of being a singer
And to be good
So I will never have to linger

I have a dream
That everyone will be equal
And for years after that
People will follow in sequel

So there we have it -
All my dreams
Some of them might be
Hard to reach, or so it seems

Just one last thing . . .
. . . What are your dreams?

Alana Dale (12)
Verdin High School

I Have A Dream

I have a dream that one day I will be a rock star.
Maybe my band will go far.

I have a dream that one day Manchester United will win the Champions League again.
Ruud van Nistlerooy, last minute from a pen!

I have a dream that one day Liverpool will get relegated from the premiership.
Then Rafael Benitez will be out on his hip.

I have a dream that one day England will win the World Cup.
Beckham will lift it high, up, up, up.

I have a dream that one day poverty, war and racism will cease
And the world will be in total peace.

I have a dream today. I'll try to let no one change my ways.

Marc Hatton (13)
Verdin High School

My Poem

My poem is about a man
Who will do anything he can
All he wants is rights for all
Even on his final call
Because death is at his door

He shows his love for me and you
Doesn't matter if animals baa or coo
People don't accept his life
Even through his struggle and strife
He is a hero, that no one can deny

Lots of others have joined his cause
Some have started then put it on 'pause'
Some care and some don't bother
Even though it affects their mother
We people do not accept that everyone is treated as equal.

Alex Thompson (13)
Woodford Lodge High School

Martin Luther King

I had a dream,
That black and whites are equal,
That love and respect are sequel,
Do you think we are less?
Do you think whites are best?
Did you have that dream last night
Where we hurt, hit and fight?
The law is on your side,
About us you lied.
I don't want to fight,
I want people to have a clear sight.
To see what people are inside,
You treated us ill till we died,
Then I woke up and looked around,
No crying, no screaming, no sound,
I drifted back to the time
When black and white couldn't dine,
We were treated different,
Just because of colour pigment,
I wanted black and white to sing,
Because I was Martin Luther King!

Alexandrea Hall-Holtom (13)
Woodford Lodge High School